Kant's *Groundwork of the Metaphysics of Morals*

T0333707

Edinburgh Philosophical Guides Series

Titles in the series include:

Kant's *Critique of Pure Reason*
Douglas Burnham with Harvey Young

Derrida's *Of Grammatology*
Arthur Bradley

Heidegger's *Being and Time*
William Large

Plato's *Republic*
D. J. Sheppard

Spinoza's *Ethics*
Beth Lord

Descartes' *Meditations on First Philosophy*
Kurt Brandhorst

Nietzsche's *Thus Spoke Zarathustra*
Douglas Burnham and Martin Jesinghausen

Deleuze's *Difference and Repetition*
Henry Somers-Hall

Foucault's *History of Sexuality Volume I, The Will to Knowledge*
Mark Kelly

Kant's *Groundwork of the Metaphysics of Morals*
John Callanan

Visit the Edinburgh Philosophical Guides Series website at
www.euppublishing.com/series/edpg

Kant's
Groundwork of the Metaphysics of Morals

An Edinburgh Philosophical Guide

John J. Callanan

EDINBURGH
University Press

© John J. Callanan, 2013

Edinburgh University Press Ltd
22 George Square, Edinburgh EH8 9LF

www.euppublishing.com

Typeset in 11/13pt Monotype Baskerville
by Servis Filmsetting Ltd, Stockport, Cheshire, and
printed and bound in Great Britain by
CPI Group (UK) Ltd, Croydon CR0 4YY

A CIP record for this book is available from the British Library

ISBN 978 0 7486 4726 2 (hardback)
ISBN 978 0 7486 4725 5 (paperback)
ISBN 978 0 7486 4727 9 (webready PDF)
ISBN 978 0 7486 8195 2 (epub)
ISBN 978 0 7486 8196 9 (Amazon ebook)

Contents

Series Editor's Preface

To us, the principle of this series of books is clear and simple: what readers new to philosophical classics need first and foremost is help with *reading* these key texts. That is to say, help with the often antique or artificial style, the twists and turns of arguments on the page, as well as the vocabulary found in many philosophical works. New readers also need help with those first few daunting and disorienting sections of these books, the point of which are not at all obvious. The books in this series take you through each text step-by-step, explaining complex key terms and difficult passages which help to illustrate the way a philosopher thinks in prose.

We have designed each volume in the series to correspond to the way the texts are actually taught at universities around the world, and have included helpful guidance on writing university-level essays or examination answers. Designed to be read alongside the text, our aim is to enable you to *read* philosophical texts with confidence and perception. This will enable you to make your own judgements on the texts, and on the variety of opinions to be found concerning them. We want you to feel able to join the great dialogue of philosophy, rather than remain a well-informed eavesdropper.

Douglas Burnham

Introduction

This book is a short commentary to accompany Kant's *Groundwork of the Metaphysics of Morals*. The *Groundwork* is a classic work of moral philosophy and the purpose of this book is to give students new to the study of philosophy an understanding of some of its central themes.

It might help the reader to first point out what things this book does *not* propose to offer: it does not offer a paragraph-by-paragraph analysis of the *Groundwork* (though it does closely follow the structure of that book and occasionally focuses on particularly important passages); nor does it present the reader with an introduction to the range of interpretive questions with which Kant scholars have to grapple; finally, it does not present an overview of Kant's 'practical' philosophy (i.e. the full range of his moral and political works). Instead, this book proposes to assist students who are coming to read Kant's *Groundwork* for the first time.

Although the *Groundwork* is a short work, it is thought to capture the core of Kant's moral theory. Kant's writing in general is notoriously difficult, and the *Groundwork* is no exception. Though short, each of its paragraphs was carefully composed and many of them are intended to convey several different and sometimes subtle points. Moreover, Kant's philosophical project is one that he thought required its own precise vocabulary, and this work is similarly full of peculiar technical terms. Finally, although the *Groundwork* contains many memorable and evocative phrases, Kant's overall literary style can be quite off-putting. Despite all these challenges to understanding the *Groundwork*, the student who does so can discover a work of profound moral commitment, sensitivity and concern for human beings. These features risk being lost in translation, and this book is intended to provide a reader with a clear, non-technical and sympathetic interpretation of some of the concerns that are driving Kant's inquiry.

There is no substitute for the experience of reading the primary text of the *Groundwork* itself, and this book is not meant as a replacement for that experience. Instead, the student should attempt to read the relevant section of the *Groundwork* first, and then turn to this book to consider some of the themes that can be found there. Then the student can return to the primary text with some of these themes in mind. Chapter 2, 'A Guide to the Text', will follow the general structure of the *Groundwork* itself, which is split into a Preface and three Sections:

Preface

First Section – Transition from common to philosophical moral rational cognition

Second Section – Transition from popular moral philosophy to the metaphysics of morals

Third Section – Transition from the metaphysics of morals to the critique of pure practical reason

There are numerous translations of the *Groundwork* available, too many to list here. The edition used in this book is the one published by Cambridge University Press in 2012, translated by Mary Gregor and recently updated by Jens Timmerman. Every edition will include small (and sometimes not so small) differences of translation. There are many excellent translations, however, and the references in this book use the so-called *Akademie* system (which refers to the German edited collection of Kant's works). The *Groundwork* begins at page 387 of the fourth volume of that collected edition, and good editions will include the reference '4: 387' in the margin of the text. Students should procure a copy that includes this standard pagination.

Finally, there is a study guide at the end of the book, which will offer brief analyses of sample essay topics and tips for writing essays on Kant's *Groundwork*. There is also a glossary of key Kantian terms.

1. Historical Context

Immanuel Kant was born in Königsberg in East Prussia (now Kaliningrad, a Russian exclave) in 1724, to a poor family. Kant studied and then worked as an unsalaried lecturer at the University of Königsberg, teaching a wide variety of topics, including metaphysics, ethics, mathematics and anthropology. He finally became a professor at the university in 1770.

During the 1770s, Kant's thinking started to undergo a profound change, which culminated in the publication of the *Critique of Pure Reason* (the 'First *Critique*') in 1781. This work marks the beginning of Kant's so called 'Critical period', and was followed by a huge range of works, including two more critiques, the *Critique of Practical Reason* (1788 – the 'Second *Critique*'), which concerns ethics, and the *Critique of the Power of Judgment* (1790 – the 'Third *Critique*'), which concerns aesthetics and teleology. Kant also produced numerous other important works in this period, including the *Metaphysical Foundations of Natural Science* (1786), *Religion within the Boundaries of Mere Reason* (1793) and the *Metaphysics of Morals* (1797).

The *Groundwork* was published in 1785 and thus is a work that stems from Kant's Critical period. In order to understand the context within which this work was produced, we must be aware of several points. Firstly, Kant's philosophical work is usually thought of as belonging to the 'Enlightenment' period in European culture. Just what the Enlightenment movement involved is a difficult question, but one of the key themes that was developed through the seventeenth and eighteenth centuries concerned the relationship between science and religion. Many Enlightenment thinkers, such as Rousseau, Voltaire and Hume, stressed the importance of the great strides made by the sciences of the time, and the potential challenge science provided to the previously accepted authority of the Church. Kant himself was an active participant in the science of the day, and explicitly characterised his work as aspiring to pursue philosophy as a science. Kant was also a man of deep religious convictions however, and many of his works involve an attempt to determine the relationship between the domain of religion and the domains of natural science, metaphysics and moral philosophy.

Secondly, Kant's own philosophy must be placed in relation to the philosophical movements of Empiricism and Rationalism (though these terms themselves are ambiguous and should be taken to offer only a rough guide to the philosophical outlooks of the time). Empiricism can be understood as a position that prioritises the knowledge that is acquired from experience, especially through the input offered by sensation (representatives include Locke and Hume). Rationalism can be understood as the position that prioritises the knowledge that can be acquired through the use of our rational capacities alone, and that does not appear to depend importantly on the information gained through the senses (representatives here are usually thought to include Descartes and Leibniz). Leibnizian philosophy had been dominant during Kant's so called 'pre-Critical' period, and the most influential philosophers of the time would have been those sympathetic to Leibniz's approach, including Wolff, Baumgarten and Mendelssohn.

Thirdly, not all philosophers offered entirely optimistic accounts of the possibility of knowledge. Notoriously, Hume's Empiricism led him to claim that many of our core metaphysical concepts – such as causation, substance and even the self – are concepts that cannot be justified as genuine ones. In the First *Critique*, Kant's defence began from an acceptance that Hume's scepticism offered a powerful challenge to metaphysics as it had previously been conceived by rationalists and empiricists alike. His response is to offer a reconception of just what metaphysics itself is. Although we will not be able to explore the details of this strategy here, there are several aspects of this reconceptualisation of metaphysics that are especially pertinent for Kant's picture of moral philosophy presented in the *Groundwork*. It begins with his so-called 'Copernican Turn', where Kant states that a crucial mistake in the history of philosophy was to think that human knowledge needs to conform to objects – rather, he thinks, objects must conform to our knowledge (*Critique of Pure Reason*, B*xvi*).

What does this mean? The meaning of the Copernican Turn has many different dimensions. In the case of Kant's theoretical philosophy, it involves the idea that even in perceiving ordinary objects through sensation, there is already a huge contribution made by the human mind in making sense of that experience. As such, the previously held distinction between reason on the one hand and sensation on the other is mistaken, since both must co-operate with the other in order for full perceptual experience even to be possible.

Another aspect to the Copernican Turn concerns Kant's opposition to what he refers to as 'Transcendental Realism'. Transcendental Realism is the name for a family of philosophical theories that have one feature in common, regarding what it is to give an explanation in philosophy. This feature is the claim that in order to give an adequate explanation of something, our representations (our sensations, thoughts, etc.) have to 'match up' to the essential features of some external independent realm. Imagine for example a Platonist who thinks that there is a special non-physical reality made up of Forms and which can be accessed only with reason's power to have insight into that world; alternatively, imagine a Lockean who thinks that reality is made up of physical matter which we can know primarily through our sensory capacities. Both of these positions are examples of what Kant would call Transcendental Realism, since both think that what it is to give a true account of reality is to use our representations to match up with some domain of things in themselves (whether a Platonic heaven or world of matter) that exist independently of the human mind.

Kant's Transcendental Idealism represents a rejection of this account of what makes a good philosophical explanation. While he believes that there *is* an independent realm of things in themselves – it is the explanatory basis of why there is anything that exists at all – he does not think that we need to have access to this realm in order to access objective truths. Rather, Kant thinks that we can refer to the representations that are produced by the mind on its own and discover rules and laws that govern what it is to be a rational being. Reference to these rules alone, he thinks, can provide us with access to objective truths. According to Kant, if we think that representations must latch on to the world of things in themselves, then knowledge itself will be impossible. However, if we think that they do not need to do this in order to give a good philosophical explanation of some concepts, and instead restrict ourselves to the domain of 'appearances', that is the physical world as it is characterised by human representations, then we can see a way in which objective knowledge, such as mathematical knowledge (and, as we shall see, moral knowledge too) might be possible.

Kant's Transcendental Idealism is controversial, however, since one of the claims of the theory is that the realm of things in themselves, although real, is not one of which we can know anything at all. Moreover, Kant identifies many fundamental philosophical questions that he claims could only be answered if we had access to that world. While Kant claims that many philosophical concepts (e.g. substance and causation) can be objectively known – since he thinks they just concern the ways in which representations relate to each other – other fundamental concepts, such as the notions of the self and freedom, concern the unknowable realm of things in themselves. Human beings themselves have two sides, he suggests: on the one hand, there is the human self as it appears in our thoughts and sensations, and this is something that he thinks we can know; on the other hand, there is the self as a thing in itself, which he thinks is the source of our ability to act freely, and this is entirely unknowable.

Kant's conclusion in the First *Critique* is perhaps less than one would have hoped for – ideally, we would surely like a proof that we *are* in fact really free. If our freedom is something that relates to the unknowable aspect of human beings, then such a proof will *never* be forthcoming. However, Kant thinks that this is the cost that one must accept, especially if one understands the benefits Transcendental Idealism brings (by explaining how objective knowledge of mathematics, causation, etc. *is* possible). What is more, by showing that our freedom is something that, if possible, relates to the realm of things in themselves, Kant shows that neither can it be *disproved* that we are free. There is here then a modest kind of response to the determinist or 'fatalist' who argues that freedom is definitely impossible and that all our actions must be entirely determined by physical causes.

Therefore while Transcendental Idealism provides answers to some philosophical questions, it takes others off the table for debate. Kant famously claims that another benefit of his theory is that it provides the same result for the topic of religious belief. Although the scientific pursuit of metaphysics shows that we cannot prove the existence of God, it does so by showing that God too must belong to the realm of things in themselves. Therefore God's existence or non-existence is not in fact a proper question for philosophy. Kant is very much an Enlightenment scientific thinker, and intensely opposed to those who would claim that the certainty of their own religious beliefs serves as a justification for intolerance of those who lack those beliefs. On the other hand though, another part of Kant's aim is to preserve a special dignity for the kind of inquiries that we might make in a church, mosque or synagogue, inquiries which he claims do not concern questions of knowledge but rather those of faith.

As we shall see, each of these themes emerges in different ways in the *Groundwork*. There is no doubt that this work is meant to fit into Kant's overall picture of Transcendental Idealism. This raises an important and difficult issue, which is whether one has to become a Transcendental Idealist in order to accept a Kantian moral philosophy. While there are many moral philosophers at work today who would identify themselves as Kantians, there are far fewer who would identify themselves as Transcendental Idealists. As we shall see, much of the *Groundwork* proceeds without any explicit appeal to Transcendental Idealism, which has raised the hopes of many that most of Kant's insights can be preserved even without committing to every part of his philosophical system. However, we shall also see that Transcendental Idealism returns in a dramatic fashion in the closing stages of the *Groundwork*, and in a way that Kant indicates is crucial to the whole project. The reader will then have to consider this question for him or herself once the entire picture of the strategy of the *Groundwork* is understood.

2. A Guide to the Text

The title of the work is *Groundwork of the Metaphysics of Morals*. The title alone indicates several things about the nature of the inquiry Kant is undertaking here. While it is obviously an inquiry into the nature of morality, it is also clear that Kant holds that morality is an area of philosophy that has its own metaphysics. If one thinks that morality might be objective, that is, that some of our moral judgements can be objectively true, then this is surely the case because there are some facts or states of affairs or *something* in virtue of which moral judgements are objectively true. Kant's inquiry will involve some kind of reference to the type of things that make moral judgements possible and as such will be involved in a kind of metaphysical inquiry. On the other hand, we can also see that this work is in some sense only a preparatory inquiry, since it is merely a 'groundwork' for that metaphysics. We are to expect then that what will be involved will be an investigation into the foundations or basic elements required for inquiry into things that can make true moral judgements possible.

Preface

Kant begins the *Groundwork* in a very formal manner, setting out a systematic division of knowledge. This formal division is important, however, since it will emerge that it can reveal some things about the way Kant conceives of ethics. The system of knowledge is one he thinks the Ancient Greek philosophers originally pursued, and which distinguishes physics (the study of nature), ethics (the study of morals) and logic (the study of reasoning). While Kant agrees that these are the main divisions of knowledge, he rearranges them into a kind of hierarchy in the following paragraph. It is worth looking at his division since it can already give us some insight both into the style of Kant's thinking and also as to the themes that will re-appear later on.

In the next paragraph, Kant states that these areas of study are fundamentally all forms of *rational* cognition. This general family of rational cognition splits up into two smaller divisions – those that have objects relating to them, which he calls *material*, and those that do not, which he calls *formal*. If one's study is merely formal rational cognition, one is studying logic. Thus Kant thinks of logic much as we do today, as the study of abstract forms of valid and invalid reasoning. When we study logic, we do not think that there are any particular kinds of *things* related to it – in fact, we think that one of the features of logic is that it is 'topic-neutral', as some contemporary logicians say – we can plug in any propositions we like and use the same forms of reasoning to test whether or not the argument is formally valid.

Some forms of rational cognition are not topic-neutral, however, and Kant describes these forms as dealing with *material* rational cognition. All this means is that these are sciences that have a particular set of objects or things with which they are concerned. Kant says a bit more than this though – he says that material rational cognition is concerned with specific objects 'and the laws to which they are subject' (4: 387). Material rational cognition can be sub-divided into two groups again, Kant says, and this depends on the type of law we are talking about. If we are concerned with the laws of nature, then we are engaged in the study of physics; if we are concerned with the laws of freedom, however, we are engaged with the scientific study of morals.

Kant therefore begins with a somewhat strange definition of ethics (or the 'doctrine of morals') as the *science of the laws of freedom*. If one were asked for a quick definition of ethics, this is not the first thing that would spring to mind. But it is helpful to ask why it is that Kant presents things this way. For example, one might notice straight away that Kant (unlike Hume, say) seems to think that knowledge is a quite systematic and orderly business, such that it can be organised in this way, with all the bodies of knowledge related to each other in a clear manner. (For many of us, this tendency to see philosophy as a whole interconnected system with a specific structure, which is sometimes referred to as Kant's *architectonic*, can seem very optimistic.) Similarly, we can see for that reason that ethics for Kant is just one branch of rational cognition. So although we will see that Kant is not a straightforward rationalist, we know that he will, nevertheless, have reason play a very central role in his moral philosophy.

We can see also that morality is deeply tied to *freedom* for Kant – furthermore he thinks of freedom as a kind of 'object' (since ethics is a form of material rational cognition), though we should not think of 'object' too literally here: Kant just means that ethics is not purely formal or topic-neutral – rather, there is a certain type of thing that it is concerned with as its special subject matter, that is, freedom. More specifically, Kant says that it is the laws of freedom that are the objects of study when we engage in ethical reflection. This is surprising in itself, as one perhaps never thought of freedom as the kind of thing that has *laws* at all. In fact, when we speak of freedom, we usually speak of it in exactly the opposite terms, as freedom *from* being constrained by any rules or laws. That is, we think that *just what it is* to be free is just not to be under any particular constraint. What, then, can Kant mean by the seemingly contradictory thought that there are laws of freedom? This question, although it naturally arises here, will not be addressed fully until the third section.

Finally, we see that Kant thinks that the study of the laws of freedom, that is, ethics itself, is a *science*. This is another aspect of ethics that we might not have thought to be the case if we were asked to define it – we might have even thought of ethics as something opposed to science. We think that we can look to biology or neuroscience or psychology to get a kind of description of why people do the things they do, but when we are engaged in ethical reflection we are inquiring as to what people *should* do or what they *ought* to do. We tend to think that ethics is a *normative* inquiry, and not a descriptive one. Therefore, when Kant thinks that there can be a practical science, he means that there is a type of inquiry through which we can find out the rules that govern what we ought to do.

Kant is using the word 'science' in a different sense than the way in which it is used today. For Kant, any inquiry is a science if it could be shown to be one that followed certain core principles that are necessary and absolutely certain, or a priori. Also, Kant thinks that a body of knowledge is a science if it is *complete* – that is, if in laying out all its a priori principles we can be sure that we have left none out. We can put these elements together and say that when Kant says that ethics is a science, what he means is that it is a type of inquiry that is governed by a limited set of a priori rational principles. We can see then that, even from the opening paragraphs, Kant reveals a lot about his picture not just of moral philosophy, but of philosophy and science in general.

Kant goes on to claim that there are laws that determine what *ought* to happen. Our common sense notion of 'law' is that of the legal sense, or of the 'law of nature' sense, such as in physics and biology. In some ways Kant intends the notion of a law of freedom to have both these meanings. In one sense, a law of freedom obviously does not work upon you in the way that gravity does – whatever the law of freedom dictates to you, you are still in a position to disregard it, whereas this is not the case with regard to gravity. On the other hand, Kant clearly thinks that the laws of freedom are a real 'object' and that they influence our decisions and actions. He certainly does not think that they are conventional, by which I mean that Kant does not think that the laws of freedom exist just because a government or group has decided or agreed at some point in history to adopt those laws. Rather, Kant thinks that the laws of freedom, just like the laws of nature, are in some sense real and eternal, and exist whether any person, group or society endorses them or not.

Kant says that moral philosophy is concerned with the laws of freedom as they relate to 'a human being's will' – but what is a human being's will? For now we should not worry too much about the exact meaning of the term, but instead think of the will in a very general way as the ability to form intentions to act. When I deliberate over what to do, that is, when I engage in practical reasoning, the outcome of that reasoning is an intention to perform an action. I may decide to go shopping, or stay in bed, or give all my money to charity, or become a professional thief – all of these are intentions to perform a certain action, or a certain set of actions. The will is Kant's term for our general capacity to form intentions to perform actions as a result of a piece of practical reasoning. Note that the outcome of one's practical reasoning is not necessarily the action itself – I may form the intention to rob a bank but fail to actually perform that action because I am impeded in some way (let us imagine I am arrested for tax evasion before I can ever rob any banks) – but I would still have formed the intention to rob banks in any case. So Kant is declaring an interest here in the possibility of there being a *science of the will*, that is, that there may be necessary rules to be discovered that tell us something about the correctness (or incorrectness) of the intentions that we form.

Again, one might worry that this is a task for psychology and sociology rather than philosophy. However, Kant's approach here is related to yet another meaning of the term 'a priori'. I said above that the study of morals was an a priori science because it involved principles that were necessary and certain. Kant also means by 'a priori', though, that they are *non-empirical*. 'Empirical' means 'relating to knowledge drawn from experience'. So when he claims that ethics is an a priori form of knowledge, Kant means that the rules that we can discover regarding our intentions and actions are not going to be rules that we have learned from our experience. When we are looking for the rules regarding how we ought to act, we will not be looking to experience from history, or from examining the rules of our culture, or from other cultures or from what experts or authority figures in our society tell us, etc.

Kant does think that ethics has to deal with all the messy detail of human interactions – he does acknowledge that it has an 'empirical part' and this part he calls 'practical anthropology'. However, Kant is clear that in the *Groundwork* he is not interested in filling in the details of his ethics, but rather in looking at things in a very basic manner, to try and identify the fundamental rules that determine what we ought to do. Since Kant thinks these rules are non-empirical, he says that we have to pursue a metaphysics that is 'cleansed of everything that might be in some way empirical' (4: 389), which means that the theory that Kant is going to pursue will abstract away from particular empirical circumstances, and thus will be very general in its findings.

One might have some lingering scepticism that there even *is* such a thing as a metaphysics of morals in Kant's sense – that is, one might doubt that, once one has taken away everything empirical to do with the reasons for which people act, there might be anything left at all.

Kant seems to begin the book on the assumption that there is no doubt at all that there *is* such a thing as 'pure' laws that govern our forming of intentions. He seems to imply this when he talks of 'the common idea of duty and of moral laws'. This is obviously an important claim regarding Kant's very starting point, so it is worthwhile taking a moment to consider what he means by it.

Kant says that when anyone considers something to be a moral truth we understand it as involving a claim about *necessity*. He gives the example 'thou shalt not lie' – which one might not in fact agree with, if one believes in the permissibility of lying on occasion. But we can imagine many such claims that most people would consent to – for example one shall not commit infanticide, or one shall not torture another human being for pleasure. Kant claims that when we think that judgements like these are true, we think that they are *necessarily* true, that is, if I think that you should not commit infanticide, I mean that you *must* not commit infanticide. In fact, when one says 'you should not commit infanticide', one means that *no one ever* ought to commit infanticide. Kant is making a strong claim here about our intuitions concerning what we think we are doing when we make a moral judgement– he is saying that when I think that something is morally wrong, I take it that it is wrong not just for me, or for my community, or for people of my generation, but that it is wrong for all people, in all communities, always. This, Kant thinks, is just what we *mean* when we say that something is morally wrong.

Kant's claim here is not that he has identified certain moral truths, but rather he is making a claim about what moral truths, if there are any, must look like. They must be different from judgements of taste or preference. If I like to have mayonnaise with my chips, I understand this to be a judgement of taste, as, for example, a preference in music, and so on. Someone may, of course, disagree with me, and perhaps for effect they might even say 'putting mayonnaise on your chips is just wrong!', but when they say this we all understand that all they are saying is that they really do not share that preference. Things are different with moral judgements, though. When I say 'infanticide is wrong' I do not mean anything like 'I really don't have a preference for infanticide' – as if the issue were just a matter of preference, and as if it might be acceptable for others to have that preference.

One certainly does not think that infanticide is a matter of preference or taste at all. When I say that infanticide is wrong, Kant thinks that I am saying that something holds 'with absolute necessity' – it holds for all human beings. In fact, Kant goes further than this, and says it holds for all *rational creatures* whatsoever. As he puts it, when we say that something is morally wrong, it is not 'as if other rational beings did not have to heed it' (4: 389). Rather, Kant thinks that if a moral judgement is true, then it describes something that every creature capable of self-consciously forming the intention to act (as I will put it from now on, every *possible agent*) must also recognise as true. This is the core of Kant's concept of *obligation* – when we recognise a moral obligation, we recognise it as something that we (*and every possible agent*) are obliged to do (or refrain from doing).

Many readers first approaching Kant's ethics find his talk of 'obligation', and especially his talk of 'duty', unattractive. 'Duty' is a word that is far less common today with regard to discussions of morality. The primary association for most students is that of authority. We imagine one has to do one's duty when one has enlisted in the military, for example. Occasionally, one hears talk of having to do one's duty to one's parents, or to one's country, but this is just as frequently thought of as an outmoded notion, referring to more authoritarian cultures and periods than our own.

It is crucial to see, though, that this is not what Kant is talking about when he talks of doing one's duty. What Kant is trying to highlight with the idea of duty is the notion of obligation, and this is tied to the idea that sometimes one recognises that one is bound to acknowledge something as true. Compare the case of mathematical judgement. When I recognise that 7 + 5 = 12 is true, I recognise that it is necessarily true. Just by grasping the concepts that are involved in the judgement I understand not only that it is true, but that it cannot be false. I want to say that, in grasping this judgement as true at all, we recognise that we are bound or obliged to recognise it as necessarily true. It is not like a judgement such as 'Moscow is the capital of Russia' – I can imagine that, although this is true, it could have been false (for a while St Petersburg was the capital of Russia, and I can imagine that it could have happened that it stayed the capital). It is different, however, with 7 + 5 = 12. Once I understand what it *means* to say that $7 + 5 = 12$, I understand that it always has been and always will be true. I can say the words 'maybe $7 + 5$ could have equalled 13' but I cannot really even understand how this could possibly have been the case.

This is another and important aspect of what Kant means when he says that a judgement is a priori – it is a judgement whose truth is understood to hold with absolute necessity. But crucially, Kant thinks that as well as mathematical a priori truths, there are moral judgements that are a priori also. He thinks that it is obvious (and that everyone thinks this too) that 'infanticide is wrong' looks like an a priori truth. When I say that 'infanticide is wrong' I do not mean that it is true for me now, but that perhaps it could have been the case that infanticide is acceptable. Our thoughts about the fact that infanticide is wrong are not like the way we think about the fact that Moscow is the capital of Russia. The way we think about infanticide is more like how we think about $7 + 5 = 12$. We think of it as being a kind of truth that must be the case and that we respect it as such as soon as we understand what the judgement even means. When Kant is talking about the 'common idea of duty', he means just this feature of our moral thinking.

There is another aspect of Kant's talk of duty that it is worth noting now, before we proceed any further. In the examples I gave above, I suggested that the more common meaning of duty nowadays is tied to the idea of respecting some authority, such as the state, or the military or perhaps one's parents. In all these cases, the authority that we have to respect is something other than ourselves. However, as we shall see, this kind of respect for authority is entirely opposed to what Kant has in mind, since for him, the only duties that one *must* obey are those duties that in some sense come from one's own self.

What does this mean though? If we hear talk of duty outside of these 'respect for authority' cases at all these days, it is often when someone is explaining a course of action that they feel they *have* to do because they feel they 'owe it to themselves' in some way. When expressing this thought, they might say 'I have a duty to myself to do this'. What does one mean when one says that one has a duty to oneself to pursue some course of action? Usually, the idea one is trying to communicate is that pursuing this course of action is necessary in order to be the person that one thinks one is, or to be the person one thinks one should be. Someone might say 'I could stay working in this job, but I really think I have a duty to myself to explore this other career' – when the person says this, she means something like 'I wouldn't really be true to myself if I stayed working in this job'. Note here, though, that she is not following a duty that is laid down by the state, or the military or her parents. In this case there is a duty, but it is one that comes from recognising something about one's own self. When Kant thinks that moral claims have a basis in duty and obligation, the duty that one is then under is not to any external person or organisation, but really is a duty to oneself.

When we are under a moral obligation we are engaged in a process of recognising that we must perform a certain action just because we would not really be true to some aspect of ourselves if we were not to perform that action. This is a radical and complicated idea, and we will return to it later on. Kant acknowledges that determining just what our true moral obligations in fact are is not an easy task. This is because human beings are complex psychological creatures who often have a variety of factors at play whenever they engage in practical reasoning. Pursuing this inquiry is important though, Kant says, because if we do not identify the proper method for telling whether or not our intentions are morally correct, it could happen that moral reasoning becomes 'corrupted' – that the reasons that we take to be correct are in fact incorrect without our realising it. A crucial aspect of moral reasoning, he says, is its self-critical aspect, whereby any time we are in possession of a morally good reason for our action, we ought to be able to tell exactly *why it is* that it is a morally good reason.

Kant expresses this with a famous distinction between *conforming to* the moral law and acting *for the sake of* the moral law (4: 390). My behaviour might match up with what is the right thing to do, but I could be engaged in that behaviour for entirely incorrect reasons. I might give money to charity, say, but only because I see that this is what people do, and I want to conform with the habits and customs of my community. But one should not give to charity just because it is the custom of the community – one should rather give to charity simply because it is the right thing to do. In this case, I have done the right thing, but only accidentally, because I used as my rule the idea of copying the behaviour of others. We can easily imagine how, if this were one's method for identifying morally correct behaviour, one could very easily and very quickly go wrong, since so often the habits and customs of society have involved pursuing *im*moral courses of action.

The idea that Kant is trying to get across is that when we form the intention to perform an action, for that intention to be of moral value the basis for our intention must be the very same thing that makes that action good in the first place. It is not good enough to perform an action for one reason when the explanation why that action is the right thing to do is an entirely different reason – our behaviour simply does not count as morally good in such a case. It is because moral deliberation works in this special way, where it concerns itself with a special kind of 'object' – that is the free will of the agent and the laws that govern it – that Kant thinks that this kind of inquiry is different from those that try to draw conclusions from assumed general features of human behaviour:

> For the metaphysics of morals is to investigate the idea and the principles of a possible *pure* will, and not the actions and conditions of human willing in general, which are largely drawn from psychology. (4: 390)

When Kant talks about a 'pure will', he has in mind the idea of an agent who is being examined not in virtue of the general psychological features that explain why she does the things she does – this, Kant says, would be more akin to a psychological inquiry. Instead, Kant has in mind special cases of when that agent deliberates, cases where the agent is motivated to perform an action because, no matter what other reasons for performing the action she might have, in this case she has formed the intention to perform that act *just because* she thinks it is the right thing to do. The 'object' of her practical deliberation here is the very idea of 'doing the right thing'.

Of course, this book is not the one entitled *The Metaphysics of Morals* – Kant wrote that later. The *Groundwork* is not concerned with spelling out the details of what the particular right and wrong things to do are in specific types of cases. Rather, it is concerned with something more basic and more abstract – it is interested in discovering the thing that makes behaviour morally valuable in the first place:

The present groundwork, however, is nothing more than the identification and corroboration *of the supreme principle of morality*, which by itself constitutes a business that is complete in its purpose and to be separated from every other moral investigation. (4: 392)

The first thing to mention is that Kant is not denying that there are more moral investigations that one could make. So one should not expect the *Groundwork* to deliver *everything* that is relevant to morality. However, the thing that it is concerned with is significant enough: the 'supreme principle of morality', the account of what moral value itself is. A second thing to note is that Kant's expression here implies that there is just *one* single supreme principle, which is a major claim in itself. Finally, and perhaps most importantly, one must note that Kant separates out two jobs that the book will complete: it will both 'identify' and 'corroborate' the supreme principle of morality.

What is the difference between these two tasks? The first task is that of identifying just what the supreme principle of morality might be. The second task is showing that there really *is* such a supreme principle of morality. We might understand this in comparison with a distinction in the theory of knowledge, where we can distinguish between the *question of definition* and the *question of possibility*. The question of definition concerns the task of identifying the nature of knowledge, while leaving it open how much knowledge we actually have, or even whether we have any knowledge at all. The next question, the question of possibility, asks the question how much knowledge we in fact have. There is a logical priority of the question of definition over the question of possibility, since in order to answer whether or not we have any knowledge, we must first have an idea of what it is that we are looking for.

In a similar way, Kant is going to pursue his inquiry in the *Groundwork* first by trying to isolate the question of a definition for morality, by identifying just what the supreme principle of morality could be, and only then will he address the question of moral possibility, the question as to whether there really is a supreme principle of morality whose authority we must recognise. The first question is pursued in the first and second sections of the *Groundwork*. The question of the possibility of the supreme principle of morality is addressed in the third section.

Kant says that he will proceed first in an 'analytic' manner, whereby he will analyse the common idea of duty and try to discover the basic parts that constitute the common understanding that we have. Once he has done that, he will switch methodologies, and proceed in a 'synthetic' manner, whereby he will build up again from those constituent parts and show how they can be traced back again to the starting point, which was our common understanding of morality. We will see as we continue how and where Kant is pursuing each of these methods.

First Section – *Transition from common to philosophical moral rational cognition*

Kant starts this section with a famous – even if not entirely clear – claim: that there is nothing 'in the world, or indeed even beyond it, that could be taken to be good without limitation, except a **good will**' (4: 393). In one sense, understanding what this means will be the task of understanding the whole book, and it is a phrase that we will return to regularly. For now though, we might ask: what is it that Kant is looking for? What is it for something to be good without limitation? Are there are any goods that are, in Kant's phrase, 'good without limitation'? To put it another way, are there any *unconditional* goods?

One might ask why anyone would want to know. It is not obvious that there *is* such a thing as an unconditional good or even why we would need there to be such a thing. It might seem to us to be a bit of a fantasy in the first place to think that morality needs such things as 'unconditional goods'. Recall though Kant's claim about moral judgement in the Preface. There he said that we all know that when we say that something is the right or wrong thing to do we recognise that it has a kind of necessity about it. The notion that Kant is trying to get across is that the idea of morality involves the idea of a kind of necessity, and that this is captured in the further idea of something being an unconditional good.

It is a little easier to get hold of the notion with regard to actions that we judge to be wrong. It is not just that as a matter of fact infanticide is wrong, for example; rather, it is necessarily wrong, in the sense that nothing could change that fact. This truth holds no matter what anyone thinks or whatever opinion someone might have now, or whatever views they might have held in the past or will hold in the future – nothing anyone might argue, and nothing anyone ever will argue, could make infanticide morally acceptable. Furthermore, when we say that infanticide is wrong, we do not mean anything like 'for civilised societies, infanticide is wrong' or 'these days, we think that infanticide is a bad thing' – when we say that infanticide is wrong we do not mean it with any qualifying conditions attached (we do not need to qualify our judgement with the conditions 'these days' or 'in our society' or 'for us'); when we say that infanticide is wrong, we just mean that it is wrong *full stop*. Infanticide is *unconditionally* wrong.

Kant's thought is that when something is morally right, or morally wrong, we can tell by seeing whether it is unconditionally so. This idea of something being 'good without qualification' is the mark of morality for Kant. His aim in this section is to uncover what possible candidates for the role of 'something that is good without qualification' are available. He begins the section with his conclusion, that there is only one thing that is suitable to play this role, and that thing is a good will. His strategy will be a negative one first of all though, and in the first two paragraphs he considers some candidates for what might be an unconditional good. Kant rejects them all, and this can help us understand what he means when he says that, in the end, it is only a good will that is an unconditional good.

Kant considers a range of things that we would ordinarily consider 'goods' and claims to show that they are not suitable candidates to serve as unconditional goods. Kant does not deny that these things are 'goods' of some sort, considering merely that they do not possess the particular kind of goodness that is distinctive of *moral* goodness. He divides these goods into two broad camps, which he calls 'talents of the mind' and 'gifts of fortune' (4: 393). Talents of the mind are things such as confidence, perseverance and other character traits. The argument Kant deploys is a simple one: if something is morally good, then there is no context or situation in which that thing might be morally bad; however, there are many situations where these character traits can be put to an immoral purpose; therefore these character traits are not themselves morally good. For example, someone might show great talents in their aim to engage in a task of genocide – they might demonstrate great organisational skill, perseverance in overcoming obstacles, perhaps even a kind of strange courage in standing up for what they believe in, since someone engaging in a genocidal endeavour would no doubt face great challenges to their beliefs from others. But that someone might have all these talents would not lead us for a moment to think that their course of action was a morally good one. The same argument holds with regard to gifts of fortune – money, power, celebrity – all of these things can be abused by those who have objectives that are not themselves morally good. If goods can be used to contribute to the performance of evil and the bringing about of harm, then those goods cannot themselves be goods 'without limitation', since they lack what Kant calls 'inner unconditional worth' (4: 393–4).

Kant then seems to claim that all the things that we might ordinarily cite as sources of happiness are at best morally irrelevant and at worst can be used to undermine moral behaviour. This might strike some as unreasonable – what is so wrong with the pursuit of happiness? Similarly, what is wrong with having the talents of mind and gifts of fortune that might lead one to happiness? In response, Kant might say that there is nothing wrong with happiness *per se* at all. If we look again at the text, what he says is that all these advantages in life can contribute to 'that entire well-being and contentment with one's condition, under the name of *happiness*' (4: 393). Perhaps Kant is speaking ironically here in saying that what people call 'happiness' they often refer to their sense of self-satisfaction with their gifts of fortune. It is a question, though, as to whether such a sense of self-satisfaction really is what deserves to go 'under the name of happiness'. We can imagine someone being incredibly self-satisfied with their celebrity or wealth, or perhaps with the state of their physical fitness – perhaps some of these people would describe themselves as happy for these reasons, but we can easily imagine those who would claim all of these benefits but still not claim that they are therefore happy.

Kant says that if we, as an 'impartial spectator', consider two individuals, both of whom are rich, healthy, well thought of, etc., one of whom has got that way through acts that are evil while the other has achieved these benefits through their morally good conduct, we feel pleased for the latter, though we do not feel the same way for the former. Why is this? If these things were themselves 'goods' then we would think the person who possessed them must therefore be good just by virtue of possessing them. But this is not the case – Kant says we think that the former person is not 'worthy' of their happiness, whereas we think of the person with a good will as someone who is somehow entitled to all the good fortune the world might throw their way and thus 'a good will seems to constitute the indispensable condition even of worthiness to be happy' (4: 393). Therefore we do not think that the trappings of happiness are themselves unqualified goods – rather, we think they are things that someone who is possessed of a good will is due in life.

There is then perhaps a common feature of these conditional goods that Kant is trying to point out with regard to these goods, and that is their potential to be acquired in a way that is not *earned* (they can be 'gifts of nature' or 'gifts of fortune', Kant says, i.e. *gifts* that we have been given without our doing anything in particular to deserve them). I may be, just by my nature, a confident and persistent individual, and I may, through some piece of good luck, have acquired wealth and power; yet we think that mere possession of these goods is not sufficient for evaluating someone's moral character. I have not done anything to earn these goods – I may have acquired happiness, but it does not follow that I have acquired 'worthiness to be happy'. But then it seems that mere *possession* of these goods is not sufficient for moral evaluation, since what we are interested in when evaluating them are the differences between the ways in which those goods are used.

Kant has no time for the idea then that having a particular characteristic (courage, integrity, health, wealth, etc.) in abundance is, or could be, an unconditional good. However, he similarly has little patience with the idea of living one's life in *moderation* as the path to goodness, for example by following a version of the 'golden mean'. As a quick refutation, Kant offers a counter-example and asks us to imagine the 'cold blood of a scoundrel' (4: 394). We might imagine an assassin calmly and collectedly going about her business. She does not get too flustered or emotional in the pursuit of her task; neither though does she get too relaxed and thereby careless. In short, she has the perfectly balanced level of composure and concentration required for the effective performance of her chosen career path. While she is definitely a paragon of moderation in one sense, all this has done is make her a more effective hitwoman. But being a hitwoman still involves doing harm to others. So moderation of goods is susceptible to the general argument scheme that Kant deploys against other goods, namely that it can be used as a means to immoral ends, and so cannot itself be something that possesses genuine inner goodness.

A crucial line of thought in Kant's argumentation against all these goods is that when we examine a particular candidate good in order to see whether it is a possible unconditional good, we see that it fails because that good can be used as a means to an end that reflects some evil purpose or aim that the agent might have. It makes perfect sense to us to attribute any or all of these goods to an individual and *then* ask the question whether or not that person is a morally good one. We might say 'Ciaran is very wealthy, but not a morally good person', or 'Patricia is a very physically fit person, but not a morally good person', etc. Similarly, we can evaluate particular actions undertaken by an individual, and characterise an action as courageous or intelligent, etc., and yet still criticise that action as an immoral one.

Kant's overarching point here is that whenever we make an evaluation of someone's *moral* character, we take it that citing these goods is never sufficient – we always have to look somewhere else in order to decide that question. Secondly though, Kant is hinting at a crucial claim for his own positive account of moral philosophy, by pointing out that when we do make a *moral* evaluation of someone, we do so by looking to the same place every time – we look to what the agent's intentions, objectives or purposes were in performing those actions. If an action demonstrated courage and intelligence, but their intention was recognisably evil, then we have no problem in making a negative moral evaluation of that person. In fact, we do not even bother to engage in any act of weighing up or balancing of those other goods against the status of the agent's intentions – it is not as if we say 'well, her intentions were evil, but her action demonstrated a lot perseverance and intelligence, and those are good qualities, so therefore overall her action was good'. In reality, there is not even a question of our performing a calculation or tallying up of non-moral goods.

There is a sense in which we recognise – as an 'impartial spectator' – that once one has identified whether or not the agent's intention was a morally good one, then that settles the question of moral evaluation. We do not even need to consider any further goods about the action or the agent's character in order to make that moral evaluation. In this way, it looks like not only is reference to these goods not *sufficient* to decide whether an agent's action was a morally good one, but that referring to such goods is not even *necessary* to decide the matter of moral evaluation.

It is for these reasons that Kant identifies a human being's *will* as the target of moral evaluation. The will is just one's capacity to form intentions to perform actions. To be possessed of a *good* will then is just to possess an intention-forming capacity that is good. But what does this mean? Kant continues in the following paragraphs to identify what he thinks are the features of the good will that make it appropriate for the role of an unconditional good. In doing so though, recall that he takes himself still to be arguing in the mode of 'common moral cognition', that is he takes himself to be making claims here that anyone can recognise as an appropriate characterisation of how we ordinarily think about morality. Having dismissed some benefits that might be thought to constitute goodness, Kant claims that a good will in fact has *nothing to do* with any benefits such as these. In fact, he goes further, and says that having a will that is beneficial or useful in this way is entirely irrelevant to whether or not it is a good will. Kant says that if there was a person blessed with a good will, but for some bizarre reason – 'by some particular disfavor of fate' – that person could never realise her good intentions in any benefits or usefulness, then that person would still be perfectly good (4: 394).

Kant's claim hinges on the importance of our identifying intentions to the ordinary run of everyday life. We must appeal to intentions in order to understand the interpretation of most human actions, not just the sub-class of actions that are objects of moral evaluation. Consider, for instance, watching a silent comedy: here we frequently appreciate the humour of the situation because we are capable of distinguishing between the intentions of the agent on screen and the outcomes or the consequences of his actions. If our hero sees that a lady has dropped her purse, and he picks it up to return it to her, only for her to turn around at the last second and, seeing him holding her purse, think that he has just stolen it, then our enjoyment of the scene as she hits our hero over the head with her umbrella is based on our understanding of how the actions that were the result of his morally good intentions were misinterpreted.

Suppose for a moment that our hero is stuck in a universe where *everything he does* is destined, through the power of some evil comedy demon, to end up being misinterpreted in this way. Every time he tries to help someone out, it is interpreted as being an attack. In this universe he is cursed with cosmic bad luck. *Every time* he tries to do something good, it turns out badly for him and for others. He tries to pick up someone's purse and ends up bumping heads with the other person bending down, and so on. The question is: if this person, from the beginning of their unfortunate screen life to the end, has caused nothing but these negative consequences, if all they had ever done was to generate injury and distress and the condemnation of others, would we say then they were an *immoral* person? Would the will of this person be then a morally bad one? On the contrary, Kant thinks that we understand in this scenario just how *good* the person really is. In Kant's evocative image, this unfortunate person's good intentions stand out even more in this context by virtue of their contrast with the universally negative consequences of their actions, and his will in this universe would 'like a jewel . . . shine by itself, as something that has its full worth in itself' (4: 394). Even in this thought experiment, where it is impossible for a person's actions to have any positive benefits for himself or for anyone else, we still somehow understand that this would not affect in the slightest our moral evaluation of that person. In fact, we have the intuition that the outcomes of his actions are somehow irrelevant to this question of whether or not he is a good person.

Kant acknowledges that this is a strange picture, since no allowance is made for usefulness either positively or negatively. He suggests we can feel more comfortable with it if we consider another argument (4: 394–5). The argument goes roughly as follows: nature has picked out various aspects of human beings for a purpose, to achieve some particular goal or other; amongst these capacities are those for immediate reactions by instinct and reflective decisions through reason; if happiness were the goal of human beings, then nature would have picked out our capacity for instinctual reactions and unreflective reaching for things, since this would be a very effective way for every individual in striving for their goal of happiness. However, we are not creatures governed by our instincts. In fact, nature has picked out our practical reasoning abilities, that is, our ability to reflect and reason about the best course of action in forming our intentions. But this capacity for practical reason *is not* the best method for achieving happiness. Therefore it must be the case that the goal of human beings' behaviour is not primarily directed just at the securing of happiness.

It is hard to know what to make of this argument – the preceding considerations Kant offers seem far more plausible. For example, we might be dubious about the very idea of nature selecting reason for this purpose or for that – we might think that nature has selected features of human beings for evolutionary reasons, that is, simply because they are beneficial for the furthering of the species. Kant was not aware of evolutionary theory in his time, of course, and one might think that all of this talk of nature selecting human reason for the purpose of morality is not very helpful. This is especially so since I think that a more characteristically Kantian point to make would be the claim that what is good is unconditionally good, and that this holds whatever 'nature' decides is helpful for the preservation of oneself or one's species. Returning to the example given before, even if for some reason it turned out that infanticide was evolutionarily beneficial (e.g. some gorilla males routinely kill young infant males, and one theory is that this is because it is evolutionarily advantageous to get rid of potential future competitors), this would not change anything about the *moral* status of infanticide for human beings – infanticide, even if originating from practices that could be considered evolutionarily beneficial, would still be unconditionally wrong.

In any case, Kant's claim – that practical reason influences the human will, so nature must have given us practical reason to influence us to be morally good – does not seem to be a particular convincing one here. Fortunately, his whole philosophy does not depend on this argument. In the course of giving this argument though, Kant outlines a very important point for his system. He thinks that what we must recognise about what we are doing when we are engaged in moral reasoning is not producing intentions that are merely good for this or that goal, or for this or that purpose. Rather, Kant says, a good will is a will that is good *in itself*, and is not a means to some other end (4: 396). The contrast between something that is good as a means to an end and something that is good as an end in itself is crucial for Kant's whole system. We can imagine that a hammer is good for hammering, and a pen for writing, or that being highly organised might be good for charity work. We saw, though, that being highly organised might good for genocidal work also. All of these things are merely good means to an end. If your end, or goal, is hammering, then a hammer is a good means to that end. If your end is writing, then a saw is not a good means to that end.

Similarly, being highly organised, which is not an example of a physical tool, but rather is a character trait, is still something that is good merely as a means to an end. Whether your end is charity work or genocide, the character of being highly organised is a good means to either of those goals. But it is not a good in itself. Rather, the trait of being highly organised is like the saw or pen – it is an effective tool or instrument for achieving certain goals. It is not as if being organised has no value at all, but rather that its value is relative to the kinds of thing one wants to achieve. For some goals, the character trait has value as an instrument for achieving those goals while for other goals (say, for example, I have a goal of becoming more spontaneous in my decision-making) it might be of less value. The general point is that what value it has is conditional on what goal one is after. As such, we tend to say that the hammer, pen and character trait of being highly organised have a merely *instrumental value* – they have a value as instrumental means to various ends.

Kant's bold claim then is that things that have only instrumental value do not have moral value. He says that he is interested only in things that are ends in themselves, not in things that are means to an end. As such, he is interested in things that have a value in them-selves, and not because they are efficient instruments for achieving something else. Recall our unfortunate comedy character – for all his good intentions, he was never able to bring about anything but distress and harm. He was never efficient at realising in an effective way any particular valuable thing. Yet for all this, Kant says, we recognised the person as a good person anyway – we recognised that although he had no traits that were of instrumental value to himself or anyone else, his actions were nevertheless not of a lower moral standing because of it. His rational will was good, and that is what counts in the identification of moral value.

One might raise a worry at this point: Kant has identified lots of things – instinct, courage, wealth, etc. – and claimed that these are not unconditional goods because they could be used instrumentally for immoral acts. But could not the same be said of our rationality? It is surely possible to use *reason* for immoral ends – why then should reason be tied so tightly to morality? Kant has not said anything yet to vindicate the idea that morality and rationality are so tightly connected, and at this stage he is only trying to prepare the reader for this claim. However, it is worth anticipating now where Kant will be going. Specifically, we should note now that Kant will allow (of course) that rational agents can use their rationality for immoral purposes; however, he will claim that it is also the case that rationality has a kind of core aspect, one that we can access in order to ask a fundamental question – *ought* I to do this action that I am considering?

I can use my rationality to ask questions quite *like* this with regard to instrumental reasoning. It is raining; I have an umbrella; ought I to bring my umbrella with me? The question I am asking myself here is whether it is rational to bring one's umbrella if one has a particular desired purpose, i.e. keeping dry. But Kant thinks that there are some types of action where we are not asking: 'should I do this if I want to achieve aim *x*?' but just simply: 'should I do this?' Kant thinks that there are some types of action that are ruled out as actions that are forbidden, or ruled in as actions that are obligatory, irrespective of what desires or purposes one has. The idea is that just as we can see that some course of action might be rational in an instrumental sense, we can *also* sometimes see how a proposed course of action might be evaluated in a non-instrumental way, and that our rationality might have a kind of non-instrumental function that can make a different kind of evaluation, i.e. whether or not we should do something irrespective of instrumental outcomes.

Thus when we are asking 'should I take my umbrella?' we are asking whether or not it is instrumentally rational to do so – it is rational if you have the desire to keep dry. If for some reason you have the desire to get wet – perhaps you like to get caught in the rain – then your instrumental rationality will answer 'no' to the question. But sometimes there are questions about courses of action that can be asked and answered without any special recourse to our further objectives or desires. Sometimes we do not ask 'is it instrumentally rational for me to do *x*?' but rather simply 'is it rational for me to do *x*?' If the question is 'should I practice torture?' the question is not appropriately responded to by saying 'well, that depends on what further purposes that would realise'.

Rather, we feel that we should be able to answer the question not by referring to our instrumental rationality, not by considering whether that act might be good *for* this or that end, but rather we should be able to answer that, *whatever* further ends one might have, one is just not allowed to practice torture. And we would hope that the answer we will have given is a rational one. So, Kant thinks, it must be the case that an aspect of rationality, one that is different from the way we use it as an instrument, must be available to us. When I ask 'ought I to do *x* if I have desire *y*?' we can understand this question as asking whether it is instrumentally rational for me to do *x* in order to satisfy *y*; but sometimes we are just asking simply 'ought I to do *x*?' In this case, Kant thinks, we are simply asking 'is it rational for me to do *x*?'

Returning to the text, Kant now turns to the concept of duty (4: 397). It has already been mentioned that the notion of duty that Kant is concerned with is very different from the idea of duty to one's parents, or to military duty, etc. The concept is vital for Kant since it allows him to draw a well-known distinction between actions done *in conformity with duty* and actions done *from duty*. The idea that Kant is trying to motivate here is that there are many actions that can end up corresponding to what is the right thing to do, but which we would be hesitant to praise the agent for doing. Again, Kant is here trying to appeal to a distinction that he thinks we all intuitively use in our everyday moral reasoning.

Kant points out that our inclinations or desires can match up or deviate from our sense of duty in various ways. In order to show this, Kant draws a distinction between immediate and non-immediate inclinations (4: 397). An immediate inclination towards an action is when one has a natural propensity to want to perform that action without any further reflection being required. A non-immediate inclination is when one might not have a natural propensity to do that act but one does have an inclination towards other things that action might achieve. So while someone might exercise because they enjoy the workout, that is, they have an immediate inclination towards it, another person might not enjoy the workout itself, but enjoys certain consequences exercise can bring, for example being slim, energetic, etc.

To illustrate the distinction, he uses three famous examples, which I will refer to as the *shopkeeper case*, the *depressive case* and the *philanthropist case*. Kant asks us to imagine one person in each of these scenarios, but for the purposes of making Kant's points clearer, I will talk about them as if he were discussing scenarios each involving two people. In each case we can see that while the actions of the two agents can outwardly match up, that is, they can manifest the same consequences or effects, there can be great differences in the practical reasoning procedures that each agent has undergone in order to form the intention to perform those actions. Kant's overall point here is that our intuitions regarding moral value do not track the outward consequences of the actions, but in fact track the inner deliberations of the agents. The conclusion they are supposed to show is that appeal to consequences is irrelevant to moral value and the single target of our moral inquiries is in fact the will or intention-forming capacity of the agent.

Firstly, imagine two shopkeepers, Joe and Angela. Both of them engage in the same practice, which is the practice of maintaining the same price for their products for every customer. Both of them have considered the following possibility: that a child or a tourist or a dull-witted person might come into their shop and that one could charge them more for their purchases than one charges the normal locals. Having considered this possibility, both Joe and Angela have decided it is better to keep the same price for everyone.

Are Joe and Angela morally equivalent agents? Kant would say that it depends – specifically it depends on what kind of reasoning they each have used in order to arrive at the rule 'keep one's prices the same for everyone'. Imagine that Angela, in reaching her conclusion, has reasoned like this: 'If I charge different prices for different people, and it gets out that I've been doing so, I'll be ruined; therefore, I'll keep my prices the same for everyone.' Here Angela has reasoned through considerations of the consequences of her asking for different amounts from different people; she has reasoned instrumentally that, if her goal is to make money, then having different prices for different people will ultimately not be a prudent way to realise that end. Angela did not have an immediate inclination to keep her prices the same, but she did have a non-immediate inclination to do so. By way of contrast, imagine that Joe has reached the same conclusion but through a different reasoning process. Imagine that Joe has reasoned as follows: 'I could change my prices for different individuals and maybe thereby make more money, but to do so would be entirely unfair, since it would not treat everyone as equals; therefore I shall keep my prices the same for everyone.'

Now let us assume that it is a moral law that everyone should be treated as equals, and that this has a valid application in not ripping off customers by setting different prices. We should say, I think, that both Angela and Joe acted *in conformity* with that moral law. The moral law says that one should treat everyone as an equal, and that is what both of them did. But only Joe did so *because of* the moral law. For Joe, the fact that it was simply unfair to charge different prices figured centrally in his moral reasoning, whereas that fact was not mentioned at all in Angela's reasoning. Thus, while Angela acted *in conformity* with the law, only Joe acted *for the sake of* the moral law. Only Joe's action was done *from* duty, from a sense of respect for what is the right thing to do.

We can see several notable things about Angela's reasoning. Firstly, she was concerned with the consequences of her proposed action. Secondly, she engaged in a piece of instrumental reasoning. Thirdly, we can imagine that the result of her reasoning was somehow contingent – it could have been the case that circumstances made it very unlikely that word of her price changes would have gotten out, and then her instrumental reasoning would have shown her that she *could* have gotten away with it, in which case she would have charged different prices for different people.

It does not seem that Joe looked at things in any kind of similar way. He did not *consider* the consequences of his action at all (there is a trivial sense in which he reasoned that the consequence of his action would be 'being unfair' but that is not really the sense of 'consequence' we are concerned with here). It is not clear that his reasoning was a piece of instrumental reasoning either – did he have any desire or end in mind when asking whether he should change his prices? Finally, it does not look like his reasoning was contingent – if it had been the case that no one would have been the wiser had Joe changed his prices, he *still* would not have done it. In fact it seems that since Joe was not considering any possible consequences at all in his reasoning, it follows that the same conclusion would have been reached with regard to all possible consequences. It seems that his conclusion was for him a necessary one – it told him what he *must* do in accordance with what is fair.

Imagine a second case, involving two people, Finbar and Liam. Both Finbar and Liam live in accordance with the following rule, 'take care of one's self and preserve one's health'. However, once again, imagine that each of these has a very different interior mental life, and has reached this conclusion through very different paths of reasoning. Imagine that Finbar enjoys life immensely, and fears that, were he not to take care of himself, he might put himself in a position where he could not indulge in life's pleasures as much as he does. Therefore, he concludes, he ought to take steps to take care of himself. Liam on the other hand, is a depressive sort. Unlike Finbar, who has an immediate inclination for life, Liam takes no pleasure at all in living, and finds it difficult to get out of bed in the morning, let alone take the steps required to maintain his well-being. Nevertheless, Liam reasons as follows: 'I have no desire for the pleasures associated with living; however, everyone must always maintain a respect for life in general; therefore, I will take steps to take care of myself.'

In both cases, once again, the same conclusion has been reached. Here though, Finbar had a natural desire to keep living and to enjoy life (one most of us share) and his conclusion was based on a piece of instrumental reasoning regarding how to maximise the most positive consequences associated with life. Liam, on the other hand, does not have this natural positive attitude. For him, a different kind of reasoning was required, one that involved appealing to the idea that neglecting one's life (perhaps to the point of self-harm or suicide) is simply wrong, and that therefore one must take steps to preserve and protect one's life.

We can see again an important difference in their reasoning. Imagine that the contingent circumstances regarding their personalities had been reversed and that Finbar had been born with Liam's negative inclinations with regard to life; had he then engaged in the same piece of instrumental reasoning, he would have concluded that it was best to *cease* living. If we assume that preserving one's life is in fact a moral duty, then we can see that Finbar's instrumental reasoning was faulty – it is only good luck that it arrived at the correct conclusion, in that here it merely conformed with duty – and he could have just as easily reasoned to an immoral course of action. The fault, Kant thinks, is that his reasoning never made mention of just what the morally right thing to do is, or what one has a duty to oneself to do.

Finally, imagine two philanthropists, Therese and Anne. Both spend each Saturday working in their local charity shop. However, once again, the reasoning each has used in reaching the conclusion that 'one ought to help others where one can' has been very different. Imagine that Therese, like many of us, gets a nice feeling when she does something good. She reasons as follows: 'It makes me feel good to help people, therefore I ought to help others where I can.' In contrast, imagine that Anne is a misanthropic type, one who cannot stand interaction with other people, and dislikes humanity in general. Her reasoning runs as follows: 'I can't bear to interact with my fellow human beings; however, it is the right thing to do to help those in need; therefore I'll help others where I can.'

Here Kant uses the same style of reasoning to reach a conclusion that many have found counterintuitive. He claims that the actions of someone like Therese have 'no true moral worth' (4: 398). Kant then seems to say that it is only through the practical reasoning of someone like Anne that the positive moral value of the actions can be attributed. It has been thought that Kant is putting forward a moral theory for repressed types who are naturally suspicious of pleasure, since it looks as if he is saying that if I enjoy doing something, then it cannot be that it is morally good! However, Kant clearly does not mean this – at this point in the *Groundwork*, he is just trying to draw out the features of the ways in which we characterise moral value, and to point out that what counts is primarily the status of the agent's intentions.

For example, some might think that there is nothing wrong with Therese's reasoning, and that there is nothing wrong in doing morally good actions just because it gives you a positive feeling when you do so. However, Kant would immediately ask us to imagine a different possible scenario: imagine that one day Therese awoke to find that her sunny disposition had evaporated, and that she no longer took any pleasure in doing good, and that now her natural disposition was in fact more like Anne's. What would Therese do then? Well, if she kept to her old rule of reasoning, then she would reason instrumentally that helping others would produce no positive feelings in her, and that therefore she should *not* seek to help others. She would have then adopted the entirely opposite rule of conduct. But, as before, we do not think that what the right thing to do is changes every time one's disposition changes. Kant does not in fact think that there is anything wrong in receiving pleasure as a result of performing morally good actions – enjoying pleasure is natural and healthy – what he is opposed to is *basing* one's moral conduct on such considerations, that is, using the consequence of receiving pleasure as a rule or guide to one's moral conduct.

There is another aspect to this last example of Kant's to which we should pay attention. It is notable in that in Therese's case, she bases what she thinks is the right thing to do on facts about her disposition, on whether she gets a positive feeling from it or not. But these are facts over which she has no control whatsoever. It is just a lucky gift of nature that she gets pleasure from doing good, just as it is an unlucky curse of nature that Anne gets no pleasure from doing good. Isn't it an odd conclusion though to think that someone's action is morally valuable even when it is motivated by something that is not really within his or her control? Again, there seems to be nothing *earned* about the morally valuable behaviour here. Therese is in a sense just doing whatever it is that she likes to do, and it just happens that what she likes to do conforms with the moral law.

Nevertheless, some feel uncomfortable with Kant's apparent claim that sympathy is a morally irrelevant response. We do normally think of sympathetic responses – say to someone's pain – as morally praiseworthy. Furthermore, we can see that sympathetic responses frequently do produce positive consequences. However, Kant's point is primarily that it does not reliably do so. We might imagine many situations where sympathy can be counterproductive (as with relationships such as parenting, for example showing sympathy for a child's punishment for wrongdoing might undermine the child's understanding of their having done wrong in the first place).

Consider the following example. Imagine that Con, who has no strong feelings for or against his fellow man, has, unbeknownst to him, had a chip implanted in his brain overnight. The chip stimulates his brain every time he does something morally worthwhile and produces a feeling of pleasure, not unlike the feeling Therese gets naturally. With enough practice, Con learns to figure out the exact kind of things that will produce the pleasurable feelings, and ultimately devotes his life to what we would recognise as morally good behaviour. Is Con a morally good person, however? Surely, Con's intentions have been formed without him *even asking* the following question: 'what would be the right thing to do?' Rather, he simply asked himself: 'what will produce pleasurable feelings?' It is just a lucky coincidence that these feelings lined up in the right way with what is morally good – indeed we can imagine that the chip might malfunction, producing pleasure only when immoral acts were performed. If Con then proceeded by the same rule – 'perform those acts that produce pleasure' – he would then have devoted himself to an immoral life.

Kant's point is that while it is natural and normal to take some pleasure in doing good, it cannot be that human beings act morally *for the sake of the pleasure*. We act morally just because we think we should, and irrespective of whether it gives us pleasure to do so. Instrumental reasoning can take forms whereby we never even *ask* ourselves the question 'what's the right thing to do?' – but that question just *is* the question of morality. Kant's dramatic examples are directed only at bringing out this simple thought, one that he thinks we all already understand and believe.

Kant addresses a worry from a religious perspective with this understanding in mind. One might think, he says, that the command of the Bible – 'love one's neighbour' – runs counter to Kant's moral philosophy, since love is nothing but a sympathetic response and Kant has ruled out sympathetic responses from moral philosophy (4: 399). Kant's reply is that the 'love' that the Bible speaks of cannot be what he calls 'pathological love', i.e. an automatic sympathetic response. The reason for this is that the demand to love one's neighbour is supposed to be a command, but this implies that we have some power to respond (or not) to that command. However, sympathetic love is merely an automatic response, and we have no control over how much we can *feel*. What we can have control over, Kant thinks, is how much respect we can show for human beings out of moral duty, and irrespective of how much or how little sympathy we feel for them – this, he claims, is a kind of 'practical love' and is something that *can* be commanded (i.e. demanded by the moral law) and so must be the kind of love referred to by Scripture.

Kant now turns to what he calls 'the second proposition' of his inquiry (4: 399–400). This is confusing, since he has not previously made reference to any first proposition! It is a matter of some interpretive difficulty to reconstruct just what the exact formulation of the 'first proposition' actually should be. It could concern the first line of the section, namely that only a good will is good without limitation, or it could concern the claims we saw earlier, that morally actions are those that are viewed as necessitated by our sense of duty. We will not pursue this tricky interpretive issue here, however, and instead proceed to Kant's consideration of the second proposition, which he states as follows:

The second proposition is: an action from duty has its moral worth *not in the purpose* that is to be attained by it, but in the maxim according to which it is resolved upon, and thus it does not depend on the actuality of the object of the action, but merely on the *principle* of *willing* according to which – regardless of any object of the desiderative faculty – the action is done. (4: 399–400)

So far, Kant has tried to show that all the possible unconditional goods that he has looked at and rejected have had the same thing in common. This is that the good in question was always something different from the type of action performed in order to secure a specific purpose, i.e. to secure that good. Wealth, pleasure, power, positive emotions, avoidance of punishment – all of these things are goals or ends that we might perform a range of different actions in order to attain. As such, what type of practical reasoning – what 'principle of willing' – we engaged upon was not of any particular importance apart from the question of how effective it was at realising those goods (or 'objects', as Kant calls them) that we wanted to achieve.

Kant is now suggesting in this second proposition that he has shown that in fact our common moral understanding is not properly captured in terms of our pursuit of these conditional goods at all. It is that other thing, the form of practical reasoning engaged upon in forming our intentions to act, that is in fact the only thing of moral importance. What counts in our moral evaluation of an agent is whether the deliberation and practical reasoning that governed their behaviour – their 'principle of willing' – was of the right sort.

Kant's position is thus a *deontological* and *non-consequentialist* one – it opposes a notion of moral evaluation performed through a calculation of expected consequences and instead claims that morally good acts, if they are possible, are ones that are based on considerations of *duty* that can be revealed through non-instrumental practical reasoning alone. One of the common features of morality that Kant thinks that this deontological picture captures is the thought that when we think something has been performed for morally correct reasons it seems perfectly appropriate to explain that just by appeal to the agent's recognition that the act was the right thing to do. It does not seem to us that we are considering the consequences of endorsing (say) infanticide when we reject infanticide as morally wrong. It seems to us that we can adjudicate on its wrongness without any appeal to the consequences here.

It is one thing to claim that we do not need to appeal to consequences or 'effects' in order to form our moral evaluations; however, it is another thing to specify exactly what it is that we *are* appealing to when we just recognise that something is, for instance, morally prohibited. It is clear that Kant thinks that one is looking to some feature or property that one's will, that is, one's forming of intentions, will manifest in this case – but what is this feature? Kant offers the beginning of his answer in his statement of the 'third proposition', which he states seems to follow from the consideration of the previous two:

The third proposition, as the conclusion from both previous ones, I would express as follows: *duty is the necessity of an action from respect for the law.* (4: 400)

The crucial notion here, it seems, is that of 'respect' [*Achtung*], though it is never made entirely clear just what respect for the law actually consists in. The notion is a complex one and we will not be able to explore it fully here. However, Kant does mention some features that might help illuminate what he might mean. Firstly, we have already seen the notion of respect at work in Kant's distinction between actions done *from* duty and those done merely in conformity with it. So, respect is just the recognition that one should do something solely on the grounds that it is the right thing to do. Secondly, we can see that respect involves the recognition that in doing the right thing we are responding to some kind of *law*. When we recognise that x is the right thing to do, we recognise its unconditional necessity, i.e. that there is nothing that could change the fact that x is the right thing to do. A rule that has this feature of unconditional necessity is simply what Kant defines as a law.

Thirdly, Kant claims that respect differs importantly from inclinations. Perhaps Kant is thinking here of what is nowadays referred to as the feature of 'direction of fit' that some think distinguishes beliefs from desires. A belief is a kind of representation that, if successful, matches up to how the world is – if I believe that Dublin is the capital of Ireland, then my belief is a good one just if that is how the world really is. If I believe that Cork is the capital of Ireland, then my belief is a bad one, and in order to make it successful, I must change my belief. A desire, on the other hand, is a representation that does not seek to match up to how the world is, but in some ways seeks to change the world so that the world matches up with it. If I have a desire that Cork replace Dublin as the capital of Ireland, then that desire is satisfied by my changing certain ways the world is. Thus when we satisfy a belief, we do so by fitting the belief to match the world; when we satisfy a desire, we do so by fitting the world to match the desire.

When we consider what it is like to feel respect for the moral law, it is clear that the representation that we are in possession of in such cases is more akin to a belief than a desire. We think that we ought to do *x* because we take it that *x* is simply the right thing to do, and in a sense that it is not 'up to us'. We do not think of ourselves as merely declaring that we would *like* it to be true that refraining from infanticide is the right thing to do – rather, we take ourselves to be *responding* to and saying something that matches up with what objectively is the case.

On the other hand, Kant notes that the representation of respect is in other ways quite like desire – in fact at one point he claims that respect is a 'feeling' (4: 401, note). This is possibly because although the feeling of respect is like belief with regard to its direction of fit, it is also the case that the feeling of respect can be a source of motivation to action, just as desires can be a source of motivation. Just recognising that something is the right thing to do can be sufficient, he thinks, for us to be motivated to perform that action, and to try and make it so that the world is changed for the better. In this way the feeling of respect has some comparable features with desires, without itself being a desire.

The notion of respect then is a complex one, and not amenable to straightforward definition. One phenomenon that perhaps resembles it is that of conscience (however, one must be careful here: for Kant, conscience and respect are in fact different things – the points made here are just for illustration). When my conscience is activated, I am motivated to perform an action (or to refrain from performing one) just by my recognition that there is some fact of the matter that I must respect with regard to those actions; however, it also seems that when one is responding in that way, the standards of one's conscience somehow come from one's own self. Kant says that unlike desires, which are stimulated by 'external' sources (for example a lack of food stimulates my hunger), the feeling of respect is 'self-wrought' (4: 401, note): it does not seem to come from any external source, but rather from one's own capacity to consciously ask oneself the question of what one should do. As we shall see, this is a theme that recurs in later sections of the *Groundwork*.

As the first section moves towards its conclusion, Kant presents the analysis that has been performed as revealing an initially perplexing situation: on the one hand, he claims to have uncovered that what we are recognising when we are aware of our moral responses is an awareness of our responding to some kind of law; on the other hand, Kant thinks he has shown that what we cannot be responding to is the content of any particular rule *per se*. This is because particular laws concern some specific content or conditional good with which they are concerned, and Kant has shown with his negative arguments that morality cannot be tied to some particular object that we might desire to pursue. Therefore it appears that morality both must be and cannot be essentially concerned with our responses to laws.

Kant uses the Aristotelian distinction between 'form' and 'matter' in order to try and resolve this tension. Imagine an analogy with a case from perception. When we see an object – say an apple – we see it as having lots of properties: colour, shape, texture, etc. However, there are differences in the ways in which these properties are perceived. We see the green colour of the apple straightforwardly enough, but we do not see the spheroid shape of the apple in the same way. It is not as if there is a blueprint 'shape' that is seen on top of the colour of the apple – rather we somehow perceive the shape of the apple through sensing its colours, that is through the act of seeing all its colour properties and the contrast with the coloured things around it. We might think that the apple both has matter (its colour) as well as a kind of spatial form (its shape), and though we can grasp both of these things when we see the apple, we grasp them in different ways.

Kant thinks that our moral rules have a certain matter and a form also. The *matter* of these rules concerns the particular 'objects' or content that the rule might be about (such as keeping one's prices the same, or respecting one's life, etc.). However, Kant claims that each of these rules also has a *form*, and they each share that form in common. As we have seen, each of these rules attempts to articulate a moral law, a rule that holds universally (i.e. it holds for *all* possible agents in all possible circumstances) and necessarily (i.e. it says something that every agent *must* do or *must* refrain from doing). Each rule involves a command of a kind that says that *everyone must always* do *x*, or that *everyone must always* refrain from doing *y*, etc. In this way, Kant thinks that he has uncovered the shared form of our moral responses in general – when we recognise that something is morally demanded or prohibited, we take ourselves to be responding to something with a *lawlike* character. The form of morality, Kant claims, is its lawlikeness.

This leads Kant to the thought that will allow the transition to the next section of the *Groundwork*. If what we are doing when we recognise the moral content of something is recognising its lawlike quality, and if we cannot identify any particular goods or objects upon which we might base our practical reasoning, then all we have to go on when asking ourselves whether or not something is the right thing to do is to ask ourselves whether the action is something that could be lawlike, whether it could have the *form* of a moral law. As Kant puts it, human beings are the only creatures that can ask themselves this question, and inquire into the *'representation of the law* in itself' (4: 401), and this offers a solution to the tension he introduced previously – since we cannot base our moral reasoning on particular objects, we can base it on the question of whether our actions could be lawlike in general:

> But what kind of law can that possibly be, the representation of which – even without regard for the effect expected from it – must determine the will for it to be called good absolutely and without limitation? Since I have robbed the will of all impulses that could arise for it from following some particular law, nothing remains but as such the universal conformity of actions with law, which alone is to serve the will as its principle, i.e. I ought never to proceed except in such a way *that I could also will that my maxim should become a universal law.* (4: 402)

Kant has spent all this section attempting to identify not particular moral rules but what he claims most people normally take to be the major characteristics of our moral responses in general. He has tried to claim that what it is like for something to be morally demanded is for it to be thought of as unconditional, for it to serve no other purpose than its just being performed, i.e. for it to be done for the sake of its being a law. Kant has not started by identifying particular moral laws but in identifying rational lawlikeness as the major characteristic of morality *per se*.

Kant claims then that it is this feature that is the crucial thing to focus upon when doing moral philosophy. When we are looking to whether an action has moral worth or not, we must look to the intentions or will of the person performing that action. But when we look at their intentions, we should not look for a special object of intention, i.e. a special class of 'goods', but rather should look at whether or not the intentions are lawlike. Have these intentions been formed in a way such that the act is being done for the sake of the moral law? Only if the answer is 'yes' are those intentions morally good. Thus it is only if someone has *a good will* that there is an unconditional good.

Kant uses the example of never making a false promise, that is, of guaranteeing to someone that one will perform a course of action (say, paying back a debt or meeting someone in the future, etc.) though in fact one has the intention of not doing so. We will look more at this example in the second section when Kant returns to it again. Kant's main aim here is to point out the difference between asking a *prudential* and a *moral* 'ought' with regard to the practice of false promising. I might ask myself whether I ought to make a false promise in the sense of asking myself whether or not it would be prudent to do so, and of course the answer here is that there must surely be some circumstances where one might gain some advantage from doing so. However, Kant claims that the question involving the moral 'ought' can be quickly answered in the negative. The quick test that Kant devises follows from the analysis he has given above: in order to figure out whether or not a particular course of action is morally permissible, one must engage in an experiment where one imagines that it is the case that it is a universal law that every rational agent performs that course of action – we imagine a world where my proposed course of action has been made lawlike.

Kant says that once we do this we see immediately that a course of action of the general type we are considering (making a false promise whenever it would be to one's advantage to do so) cannot be make lawlike in this way. The claim is that once we engage in this thought experiment, we see that we incur a kind of rational incoherence. In the world that we have imagined, *everyone* has the intention to make false promises whenever it will be in their interests to do so. Kant then says that in this imagined world the very practice of promising would be either futile or non-existent:

Then I soon become aware that I could indeed will the lie, but by no means a universal law to lie; for according to such a law there would actually be no promise at all, since it would be futile to pretend my will to others with regard to my future actions, who would not believe this pretense; or if they rashly did so, would pay me back in like coin, and hence my maxim, as soon as it were made a universal law, would have to destroy itself. (4: 403)

It might look at first as if Kant is merely offering a more ornate form of prudential reasoning here, and claiming that when we make our rule of action lawlike (when we 'universalise' it) we see that it would not be very prudent at all to adopt the false promising rule. However, it is important to see that this is not Kant's intended reasoning here. His claim is not that we see in the imagined world that it would not be advantageous for us to make a false promise; rather, we are to see that in the imagined world it would not be *rationally coherent* for us to do so, because we have imagined a world where that rule just does not make any sense. Thus Kant thinks that this quick procedure is a way of figuring out whether something is morally acceptable or not by means of an operation or test that reveals whether it is internally coherent in accordance with the demands of our practical rationality.

This is Kant's way of leading us to the concluding thought of the first section – what it is for something to be unconditionally good, then, is for it to be something where the type of act is performed without consideration of the benefit the act might achieve but whether the act is one that can be recommended as a universal law. Kant's argument in this section has been to try and show that this unusual thought is actually what best characterises our common moral responses. With this conclusion in hand, Kant can move on to the next section, which explores the various ways in which the idea of moral truths as universal moral laws can be explored. He thinks that there is a natural transition from the first to the second section, since he has begun by examining only what he takes everyone to accept already as general features of our moral thinking. From that starting point he has reached this claim regarding the role of universalisation and practical rationality. Thus in the following section he will examine more the claims that are involved with this notion of the 'supreme principle of morality'.

Interestingly, Kant claims that what he has already provided is in some sense sufficient for making our way through the world. We can in most cases figure out what the right thing to do is through our ordinary capacity to tell right from wrong. As he himself acknowledges, this raises the question as to what further use there is for philosophy. I may not know exactly how the mechanics of morality work or what they are based upon, but I might nevertheless use my ordinary grasp of the difference between right and wrong effectively in most cases. The reason why more philosophy is required is because Kant thinks that human reason has a natural and unavoidable tendency to undermine itself and trick itself into thinking that false values are valuable. While our ordinary moral responses are on their own sufficient in most cases, we need to be on guard that our own reason has not undermined itself through this habit of 'natural dialectic' (4: 405). Some philosophical examination of the basis of morality itself and how it might be possible is then required in order to act as a kind of corrective against reason's own tendency to mislead itself.

Second Section – *Transition from popular moral philosophy to the metaphysics of morals*

The first section of the *Groundwork* was directed towards convincing the reader (a) that there is a distinct concept of morality conceived merely as the right thing to do; (b) that this concept is not properly captured by the notion of 'whatever produces the best consequences'; (c) it *is* captured by the notion of 'duty'. Kant begins the second section by worrying about how much this really shows. One could accept all of (a), (b) and (c) but still deny that human beings in reality ever manage to act morally. Kant continues his first task of the 'identification' of the supreme principle of morality in the second section, leaving the task of its 'corroboration' to the final section.

Kant considers the ways in which the concept of morality itself might relate to our experience and accepts what some might think of as some startling sceptical thoughts. He admits, for example, that it is impossible to tell whether in any given example of an agent apparently acting out of duty the agent really is acting out of duty. It might be, he concedes, that the agent might be acting out of some other motive and that it is impossible for anyone (even the agent herself) to tell which it is (4: 406–7). Consider an example of someone appearing to perform a charitable act. It is of course possible that the person is acting out of what they take to be their moral duty, that is, to help those in need; however, we cannot rule out the possibility that they might equally be motivated by the psychological desire to be thought of as a charitable person. It might be the case that their motivation is ultimately about some benefit they think the charitable act might bring themselves, even if the psychological desire is a subconscious one of which they cannot even themselves be aware. Although Kant does clearly think that acting from duty and out of respect for the moral law is in some sense a distinct kind of motivation, he does not deny that on any given occasion one might be deceived as to whether what one is feeling is in fact respect.

While Kant accepts this pervasive *fallibilism* concerning correctly identifying an agent's true intentions (even including our own intentions examined through introspection), he does not think this on its own generates a further, deeper *scepticism* about morality in general. It does not follow from the fact that we cannot know for sure whether any given case is an example of moral action that there is never any moral action. Consider a scientific analogy – imagine that a hypothesis that something is the case is theoretically demanded by our current scientific theory. We then proceed to try and prove it by conducting some experiments. However, we find that although the results of the experiments support the hypothesis, it is always the case that the result of the experiment in question could have been produced by some other factor (for example, something about the nature of our scientific equipment means that we will always get the same result, etc.). We cannot tell, therefore, from a given experiment whether or not it confirms the hypothesis in question or whether it is the result of some other factor. However, it does not follow from the fact that the experiments might not confirm the hypothesis that the hypothesis is therefore wrong. It merely shows that looking at particular examples will neither prove nor disprove the scientific hypothesis.

Some of Kant's predecessors (such as Hobbes perhaps) would have argued that for any particular given example of apparent moral action, we cannot tell whether it is in fact done out of a sense of duty or whether it was not done out of some deep self-interested desire, or 'self-love'. One might then have concluded that there is *no such thing* as acting out of a special kind of moral motivation and that all our actions are simply motivated by self-love. Kant's point here is that even if it is true that we cannot tell whether any particular action is done out of morality or self-interest, this does not show that there is no such thing as genuine moral motivation. It just shows that looking at examples for conclusive evidence of a theory is not the way to do moral philosophy.

Furthermore, it is not as if such sceptical philosophers thereby denied the coherence of the very concept of morality – on the contrary, they acknowledge that the *concept* of moral motivation out of a sense of duty, etc. *is* coherent. Rather, they make a certain claim about human nature, namely that human beings do not live up to this standard. Human beings, they claim, are a sort of creature such that their motivations are always merely inclinations (such as the inclination towards self-interest) and that their capacity for reason is only ever an instrumental one, a tool for figuring out the most effective way for realising our inclinations. What they thought was impossible, and what Kant will try to show *is* in fact possible, is that deploying a concept of specifically moral action is an essential part of what it is to be a practical rational subject, i.e. an agent capable of practical reasoning. Although we will never find any individual example that constitutes knockdown evidence that we are moral agents, Kant will show that such a conception is theoretically demanded just in order to conceive of ourselves as rational practical subjects in general.

One might draw an analogy with Kant's opposition to Humean scepticism here. Hume had argued that only concepts that can be traced back to some received sensations are genuine concepts. However, he then showed that some fundamental concepts, such as the concept of causation, do not have received sensations as their origin. He concluded then that the concept of causation is for this reason illegitimate. Kant opposed Hume's analysis, but he did not do so by identifying a special kind of sensation that might account for the origin of the concept of causation; rather, he denied Hume's initial claim that only concepts that can be traced back to received sensations are legitimate. If we allow that our minds might legitimately *contribute* some concepts in order to make experience possible, Kant claimed, then we can identify a sense in which the concept cause might be legitimate.

Similarly, Kant does not want to fight the empiricists' account of our moral concepts on their ground. He accepts that we will not find through observation or introspection evidence of any special kind of inclination that will account for the concept of morality itself. Rather, as we shall see, Kant is rejecting a model of philosophical explanation whereby we look to experience (including the inner experience of introspection) as the only source of objective and legitimate concepts, and is recommending instead that we look to the rational resources of the subject as a possible source of such concepts. If morality is a priori and objective, as Kant thinks it is, and if this means that we cannot prove it to be so through the experience of examples, then it should be the case that we cannot find any special experiential evidence of the concept of morality. If morality is a priori and objective then we will have to show its possibility in some other way.

Another fundamental insight that Kant considers concerns the relevance of experiential evidence to our moral concerns. We might, he concedes, allow that not only can we not tell whether or not an action has been done from moral motivation or not, but it might also be the case that no moral action has *ever* been performed, that is, that all the apparently moral actions that were ever performed to date were done out of self-interest (4: 407–8). Isn't this just conceding the point to Hobbes? No, says Kant, and the reason why it is not concerns understanding the very nature of moral philosophy. When we are asking what the morally correct thing to do is, we are asking what *ought* to happen. It is the case that it is very difficult to determine in any particular circumstances that someone has done something because they thought they ought to do it and not simply because it suited their interests to do it. However, not only that, but even if we presume that every human being in the history of mankind only ever acted out of their own self-interest, it still remains the case that it is a distinct question as to what they *ought* to have done and by extension what *we* ought to do both now and in the future.

Even if all human beings have acted out of self-interest, this does not provide an excuse as to whether *you* ought to act out of self-interest. Kant uses the example of friendship (4: 408) – even if all friendship to date has been merely examples of people co-operating with each other for their own benefit, that fact would not give you permission to befriend people just to see what benefits befriending them might bring you. If you are someone's friend, you ought to be their friend sincerely and for the sake of the value of their friendship, and without calculation of what benefits or disadvantages it might bring.

In general, Kant's point is against taking any facts gained from experience as themselves capable of telling one what ought to be done. If through experience one discovered that slavery had always been approved of, or that all friendships had always been based on self-interest, it would still be the case that one ought not to enslave other human beings, or base friendships on what benefits friendship might bring. Kant thinks that if we think there is any such thing as morality at all, then it is clear that facts about what people have done, or what they are likely to do, are entirely irrelevant to figuring out the answer to the question 'what *ought* I to do?' When Kant says that the notion of 'duty as such, prior to all experience, lies in the idea of a reason determining the will by a priori grounds' (4: 408), he means just that the question of what I ought to do is one that I must try to answer by means of my rational capacities and without any appeal to what has been done in the past or what is likely to be done in the future.

Kant goes on to make a further point about the use of examples, which follows on from his criticism of experience-based moral philosophy in general. Specifically, he wants to block the idea that there might be one example that does suffice as a standard against which all other moral actions might be compared, and that is the example of God's goodness (4: 408–9) (this would, of course, be an example which most of us only have experience of via the testimony of Scripture). Kant wants to block this possibility with a generalised argument schema against all attempts to derive a standard or norm from an example or set of examples. The argument is simple: in order to recognise an example to use as the standard for moral behaviour, one must see that it is an example of goodness. Yet in order to do *that*, Kant thinks, we must already compare the example to a standard of goodness that we already possess. Therefore, in order to look at examples we must already possess a standard of morally correct behaviour. Kant says that the very idea of God is nothing but the concept of moral perfection added to the idea of an agent, so that in looking to the example of God we are already, so to speak, citing the idea of moral perfection that we must already possess. Kant is here perhaps trying to block a response that this suggestion might be heretical – he does not want to say that God must obey the moral law because the latter is a higher law, rather he wants to say that God must obey the moral law because he is in some sense an inherently moral being, that he is of the same nature as the moral law itself.

Kant's description of the moral law's 'purity' then means nothing more than that it does not derive from particular examples that we may have experienced, or from theories predicting what we think human beings are likely to do. Sociology, psychology, neuroscience, evolutionary behavioural studies and economics can all tell us an empirical story about why we behave towards each other in the ways that we do, but none of them, Kant claims, can tell us whether or not we are *right* in behaving in the ways that we do.

Kant thinks that all genuine moral judgements include an 'ought' and that the proper way to think of this 'ought' is as kind of 'must' – it involves '*necessitation*' (4: 413). When I say that I ought to visit my mother in hospital, if I really think I should then I view myself as being under a kind of obligation. It is not just that it would be a nice thing to do – if it is a moral matter, then it is something that I think that I must do. For Kant, any rule that determines what must happen is properly described as a *law*. Therefore it follows that if there is any such thing as genuine moral judgement at all, then we have to think of there being something like *moral laws*. Rational agents are the only creatures who can obey these laws, he thinks, because rational agents are the only creatures who can become self-consciously aware of them, and becoming aware of them is all that is required in order to be able to see them as binding upon oneself. He expresses this in a well-known passage:

Every thing in nature works according to laws. Only a rational being has the capacity to act *according to the representation* of laws, i.e. according to principles, or a *will*. Since *reason* is required for deriving actions from laws, the will is nothing other than practical reason. (4: 412)

There is a sense then in which human beings, as rational agents, exist in two worlds (Kant will use this kind of talk explicitly in the third section of the *Groundwork*). As physical beings, we exist in accordance with laws of nature (such as gravity, for example) with which we have no option but to comply. On the other hand, as self-conscious and free rational agents, we are subject to the laws that determine what we ought to do. These laws, unlike gravity, only affect us insofar as we are capable of thinking about them – thus we can only act in accordance with the 'representation' of moral laws. Another difference between natural and moral laws is that while we cannot help but act in accordance with natural laws, we can in fact *fail* to act in accordance with moral laws – we can fail to do the right thing. This is a crucial feature of morality, since part of what we *value* about doing the right thing stems from its difficulty, from the constant possibility of one's failing to do the right thing. In contrast, we do not think there is any special value in consistently managing to obey the law of gravity.

Kant's talk of laws is crucial since he thinks only this can capture the proper account of obligation that moral philosophy requires. As already mentioned, when one recognises that one has an obligation, there is a natural inclination to talk about that moral responsibility in terms of *necessitation* – we speak of it being something that we *had* to do, or say that we had no option but to do that thing. When we speak in this way though we are obviously not talking about physical necessitation – when one says that one had to visit one's sick mother, one does not mean that there was a physical force compelling one to do so. Rather, we think of ourselves as compelled by some non-physical source of necessitation. Furthermore, we would not find it strange if someone were to state 'I must visit my sick mother, but it might not happen'. When someone says something like this we can understand them as saying that they have a moral obligation to do something, but that there are causal factors that might prevent this event from occurring. As Kant pointed out when introducing the topic of moral philosophy, it is the study of rules determining what ought to happen but which frequently does not happen (4: 388). So Kant's account is one

that will ultimately be about how human beings are the kind of creature that can respond to the rules that govern one domain (the moral)
which demands that something *must* happen, while at the same time
also belonging to another domain (the physical) where the rules that
govern that latter domain can make it so that thing does *not* happen.

Kant then will have to offer us a story about how *this* is possible,
about what it is that goes wrong when we *fail* to act in accordance with
moral laws. His story is that human beings are not *perfectly* rational
agents, in that we are creatures with more than one source of motivation. We can be motivated to act purely from our rational capacities,
which if done correctly will guarantee that we are acting morally.
However are also motivated to act out of our desires and inclinations,
and when we follow this source of motivation, it is not at all guaranteed that we will do the right thing (as we saw in the previous section,
desires might sometimes motivate us to do the right thing, but then
only accidentally, and we then merely 'conform to the moral law'). So
Kant's account of moral failure is that we are failing to pay attention
to the rational side of our moral motivations and allowing our desires
and inclinations to be the source of motivating what we decide to do.

When we recognise that a representation is telling us something
that we must do, we recognise what Kant calls an *imperative* (4: 413).
Imperatives though can come in two fundamentally different forms,
and these forms correspond to the two sources of motivation that
make up human beings' ability to act. He calls these *categorical* and
hypothetical imperatives (4: 414). When we are following our rational
nature alone, it can issue commands to act in a certain way – these
are categorical imperatives. When we are following our inclinations,
we do so by following commands that tell us the best way to satisfy
those inclinations, and these he calls hypothetical imperatives:

Now, all imperatives command either *hypothetically*, or *categorically*. The former
represent the practical necessity of a possible action as a means of achieving
something else that one wants (or that at least is possible for one to want).
The categorical imperative would be the one that represented an action as
objectively necessary by itself, without reference to another end. (4: 414)

There are some things to note here. Firstly, just because we are sometimes motivated by inclinations does not mean that reason is entirely

out of the picture. On the contrary, human beings are the kind of creature that can always use their rational capacities as a means to an end, namely, the end of satisfying those inclinations.

We are, however, also creatures that can act just by considering what our rational capacities for practical reasoning on its own tell us to do, and when we do this we are not using reason in a means-end kind of way (we are not using reason instrumentally) but are using reason in a way whereby it does not have any particular end or goal in mind. When reason is functioning like this it does not produce rules such as 'if you want to achieve goal *x*, then pursue course of action *y*'; it produces simpler rules, such as 'always pursue course of action *y*'. When our rational capacities are functioning in this way, Kant says that they produce *categorical imperatives*. (From here on, I will follow a common convention in talking about Kant's moral philosophy and draw a distinction between 'categorical imperatives' which are the individual moral commands that we might realise through acting from duty – such as 'never make a false promise', 'help those in need where possible', and so on – from the 'Categorical Imperative' which refers to the procedure or test that we have already seen introduced at the end of the first section and which concerns the process of seeing if our rule for a course of action is universalisable. This latter meaning of the Categorical Imperative sometimes gets shortened to the 'CI-test' and I will use this abbreviation also. Therefore, the CI-test is a procedure or operation, the outputs of which can be individual categorical imperatives.)

We can finally note one further aspect of Kant's way of talking of imperatives. As we have seen, Kant allows that there are all kinds of 'goods' but that these goods can ultimately be similarly classified into two broad categories. There are the goods that attach to hypothetical imperatives, which I will call *instrumental goods*, and which are identifiable by being something that is *good for* something else (e.g. a knife can be good *for* cutting, being generous can be good *for* the purpose of getting people to like you, etc.). He holds that the rules attached to the realisation of these kinds of goods do not even involve the question of their *moral* value – Kant says that the rule a doctor might adopt in order to cure someone and the rule a poisoner might adopt in order to kill someone can be equally 'good' in this 'good for' sense (4: 415).

But neither of these rules is thereby evaluated in terms of their *moral* content.

Not even happiness, Kant thinks, can serve as a guide to moral conduct. Although he holds that it is a universal truth that all human beings strive for their own happiness, the rules that they adopt are adopted instrumentally, as a means to the end of securing happiness. As such, rules regarding happiness can only generate hypothetical imperatives. Alternatively, Kant thinks that there are rule-like imperatives that are not to be understood as instrumental rules, but that there are things that we recognise as worth doing without considering any question of whether they have any further instrumental value. We can recognise the rule that is expressed by a categorical imperative as *good in itself*. Only this imperative, he claims, 'may be called that of morality' (4: 416).

Kant has a further argument here, one that harks back to his discussion of happiness in the first section. He claims that the concept of happiness is indeterminate, and that one cannot offer a specification of exactly what we mean by the concept of happiness such that we might then generate some hypothetical imperatives that would tell us how to go about achieving it. He claims that if one thought that something such as 'being rich' or 'living a long life' were offered, it might turn out that the path one took in order to become rich or to live for a long time ended up bringing about unhappiness. If the concept of happiness were specific enough for us to formulate an imperative concerning how to achieve it, then – perhaps – that imperative would have the categorical status of what Kant calls a 'command' (4: 418), i.e. it would tell us that we *must* do that thing.

This seems to make sense – we all desire our own happiness, and if we were faced with a specific rule that would guarantee that we would acquire that happiness, then it would surely seem to us that we have to obey that rule. But Kant thinks that 'happiness' is just not a specific concept at all, and so there will never be any set of specific imperatives that we have to obey in order to achieve happiness, and so no specific *categorical* imperative involving happiness as an end can ever be formulated. But since morality just concerns categorical imperatives, then it seems that the concept of happiness has little to do with the question of what we ought to do. (It should be noted that Kant has a complex account of the relation between morality, happiness and religious belief, one that he returns to in later practical works, such as the *Critique of Practical Reason* and *Religion within the Boundaries of Mere Reason*. For the purposes of the *Groundwork* though, as the inquiry into the basic foundations of morality, Kant is willing to put the positive role of happiness to one side.)

We can perhaps reconstruct a quick argument along these lines. Morality is a system of either hypothetical or categorical imperatives. If it is a system of hypothetical imperatives then there must be some goal or end to which those imperatives refer. That end cannot be happiness, for the reasons outlined above. Neither, however, can it be anything else – there are no other goals or ends that everyone will universally strive after. Human beings have various desires and do not all share the same specific ones. A hypothetical imperative will only be binding on a person so long as they have the desire for that specified end. Alternatively, we might have the desire for that end, but decide that it is not worth following the rule in order to get it – as Kant puts it 'we can always be rid of the prescription if we give up the purpose' (4: 420). But morality is not like that. By moral imperatives, we mean just the ones that we cannot give up whenever we feel like it. Therefore, morality cannot be a system of hypothetical imperatives that refers to a general end, such as happiness, or any more specific end. It must therefore be a system of categorical imperatives.

It was mentioned earlier that for Kant moral obligations will turn out to be ones that one recognises by virtue of exercising or operating one's own reason, and that this contrasts with the idea of duties to some external thing, be it a person or community or organisation or institution. One aspect of this thought is that Kant needs to explain how moral demands can be *absolutely* or *unconditionally* necessary. We need a way of explaining how moral demands can be understood by the agent as *categorically binding*. Imagine that one joins a club whose rules state that one has to attend a meeting every Tuesday evening. It is binding then on all members that they attend the Tuesday meetings. Of course there is always a sense left over in which attending the meetings is not binding: I could simply decide to stop being a member of the club. For non-members, the rules of the club are nonbinding. So there is a sense in which the necessity of the rules is not absolute but conditional – if one is a member of the club, then one must attend the Tuesday meetings, but if one is not, then one need not attend. We can see also that this is reflected in how an agent who is a member might go about explaining why the rule is binding upon them. If someone were to ask them 'why must you go to the Tuesday meeting?' the reply would be 'because it is one of the rules of the club'. If they were to persist and ask 'but do you *have* to go?' the appropriate response would be 'yes, if I want to remain a member of the club'. So there is a sense in which one does not see oneself as *having* to follow the rule – one only has to follow the rule *if* one has the desire to remain a member of the club.

But we can see now that this means that the explanation of why the rule is binding upon the person, and why they see it as binding, involves making an appeal to their desires. It is only because the person has the relevant desire, that is, to be a member of the club, that they view themselves as being under the sway of the club rules. However, just because the authority of the rules is conditional on having the relevant desires, we can make sense of the idea that the rules are no longer binding upon one if one decides to opt out from the club – if the person no longer has the desire, then they are no longer bound by the rules.

This is one of the reasons why Kant thinks that all real obligations – that is, all genuine moral obligations – must come from oneself. Any obligation that one has to an external authority, whether it be a club, a social group or an institution, and so on, will only ever be able to generate rules as hypothetical imperatives, because the necessity involved will always be a conditional necessity. An obligation to some external 'ground' will always involve merely conditional necessity, Kant thinks, because seeing oneself as under the authority of that external ground will always contingently depend on one's desiring to be under the authority of that external ground. I might think that I should pay my taxes because I wish to be a good citizen, or because I wish to avoid the punishments that can accompany not paying tax, but then the reason why I pay my taxes really comes down to the fact that I want to be a functioning member of society, and paying one's taxes is one of the rules involved in being a member of this particular club. One might respond that one is born into a particular society, and to that extent has no choice as to whether or not one is a member of that society. Of course this is true, but that is really just a matter of practicality. It might not be easy to opt out of society altogether, but one nevertheless can make the free choice to try and do so if one has that desire.

The important point to note is that Kant believes that there are aspects of one's existence that one cannot choose to opt out of, such as one's humanity, and more generally, one's freedom and practical rationality. Whatever I choose to do or not do, I must always view myself as a free agent with the power to deliberate and form intentions to pursue certain actions. There is then a very basic type of club, the club of free rational agents, which no one can opt out of. I might moreover claim that if I am opting out of anything, that activity *itself* is one that is the result of a piece of practical reasoning, as an intention to act that I freely formed. But what one cannot do is opt out of being a freely choosing agent altogether.

What Kant is trying to show is that there are rules that govern being a member of the club of free rational agents, and these rules are the ones that we can and must look to in order to discover what our genuine moral obligations are. The duties that we have are not to some external authority, but rather are in one sense duties to ourselves, since they are arrived at just by our recognition that we fundamentally belong to the club of free rational agents. In identifying the rules of that club, we are really just following the rules that decide what it is to be a free rational agent. Thus, Kant thinks, in being moral, we are engaged in the activity of expressing just what kind of creatures we in fact are.

In my using the analogy of following the rules of a club, and suggesting that Kant wants to identify the club that we cannot help but be members of, it might be thought that the fundamental club of which we are members is the club of human beings. Yet Kant carefully denies this. Our fundamental club is not actually that of human beings, but that of *rational beings* (4: 408), i.e. agents with the free will to perform actions as a result of some rational deliberation. It is of course possible that there could be some rational agents other than human beings. If our moral rules attached to us simply by virtue of our humanity, then we might imagine that aliens, for example, are not obliged to follow those same rules. If, as is the case with so many science fiction books and films, aliens decide to follow a course of the enslavement or genocide of the human species, it would be the case that we would not be able to condemn that behaviour as wrong, since the aliens are only breaking the rules of the club of human beings, a club to which they do not belong.

For Kant, this kind of reasoning would be absurd (not that he imagined such science fiction scenarios!). As we have seen, the very idea of morality, he thinks, is that it is objective: there cannot be one rule for you and one rule for me, or different rules for different cultures or generations. Similarly, there cannot be one set of rules of behaviour for human beings and another set for non-human rational beings. The rules of morality do not hold merely on condition of belonging to one species of rational agent rather than another. They do not have conditional necessity but rather they possess absolute necessity, since when I am talking about moral rules then there is a sense in which it would be incorrect to put my rules in the form of an 'if . . . then' formula. The rule is simply 'murder is wrong' and this holds for all possible rational beings, in all possible circumstances.

One might resist this line of thought and ask whether we might not still put such rules into an 'if . . . then' formulation. Might we not say something very general, such as 'if I am a rational agent, then murdering is wrong'? I think Kant would in some sense allow that we can do this. But Kant has set the discussion at such a high level of generality that it is unclear who we might be referring to when we consider possible agents who *are not* rational free agents and yet are still *moral subjects*. I can imagine that I might be an alien, but I am still an agent capable of free will and self-conscious rational deliberation. I might imagine myself to be another kind of animal, one that is not capable of self-conscious rational deliberation, but in that case I would not be a creature even capable of asking myself the question 'what ought I to do?' We do not hold such animals to be morally responsible for their actions just because we do not think that they are the kinds of creatures that are capable of self-conscious reflection on what the correct course of action might be. Kant's strategy then is to ask about the most general characterisation of the club that we find ourselves in, which is the club of agents who are capable of asking themselves the question, 'what ought I to do?' – this club is more fundamental than the club of human beings, so the answer to the question cannot be based on any particular facts about what it is to be a human being. (As we shall see, Kant will return later on to discuss our 'humanity' in a positive sense, but then he will mean it to refer to this general nature of being a free rational agent, and not to the biological species of human beings.)

Returning to the text, Kant here returns to a crucial distinction, that between *maxims* and *objective principles* (4: 420, note; Kant briefly alluded to this distinction in the first section also, see 4: 400, note). It is a matter of some debate as to what exactly Kant thinks maxims are, but here he distinguishes them as rules that are the basis upon which an agent acts, as distinguished from an objective principle, which is the basis upon which an agent ought to act. Perhaps one way of thinking about the relation between them is that an agent's behaviour is moral if the maxim which she adopted ('I ought to perform action *x*') is in fact identical with what the moral law commands (that is, the maxim she has adopted for her action is in fact what she ought to be doing). Of course, as we have seen, it is possible that one's maxim might by good fortune simply conform with what the moral law commands, and this is not sufficient.

Kant thinks that he can answer the question of definition, that is, what a supreme principle of morality might be, just from considering 'the mere concept of a categorical imperative' (4: 420). We will have to see what it means to figure out a principle (Kant here refers to it as a 'formula') just from the concept of a categorical imperative. We have already seen some features of what it is for something to be a categorical imperative: it must be a command to perform (or refrain from performing) some action; it must apply with unconditional necessity; it must not be referred to any particular end or purpose or goal; it must be objective, etc. Kant thinks that just by reflecting on what it would be for a maxim (i.e. a rule expressing some plan of action) to be adopted out of respect for the moral law, we can identify a definite procedure that one would have to adopt.

It is likely that Kant feels that his analysis of the CI-test should be able to convince an opponent, one who might initially have held that all apparently moral maxims are nothing but hypothetical imperatives – rational rules for achieving some desired end or purpose – in disguise. How does Kant hope to win over such an opponent? A first aspect of his strategy is the recognition that even the opponent must acknowledge what we might call the *authority of rationality*. The opponent might think that morality is in fact nothing but a system of hypothetical imperatives, but she would at least acknowledge that on such a conception of morality and reason, she must hold that those hypothetical imperatives are regarded as adequate rules, i.e. *good* instruments for achieving one's purposes, just because they are *rational* ways of realising one's desires. The opponent does not think that rationality *per se* is irrelevant or unreliable – on the contrary, she must hold that rationality is in some sense decisive here in determining the tools for realising one's desires. Reason has a kind of *authority* that is manifested even within our use of hypothetical imperatives.

The second aspect of Kant's strategy against his opponent is that she must acknowledge what I will call the *universality of rationality*. This claim amounts to nothing more than the idea that if agents take themselves to be acting rationally, then they take it that their reasons for acting in the way they do could be recommended to *anyone* in similar circumstances. If I think that I ought to bring an umbrella in order to stay dry, I must take it that this reasoning could make sense to any possible agent. Of course, someone might not *want* to keep dry, and so then that person might then not *want* to adopt that hypothetical imperative, but in that case one would at least acknowledge the following as correct: *if I had* wanted to stay dry, then bringing an umbrella would have been a good way of going about it. When a hypothetical imperative is a genuine one *everyone*, irrespective of his or her desires, must recognise it as such. Reason then also has a kind of *universality* that is also manifested even within our use of hypothetical imperatives.

Alternatively, one might disagree with the hypothetical imperative because (say) one thinks that in certain circumstances it is too windy for an umbrella to be effective against the rain. But notice here that if one wanted to deny that the hypothetical imperative is a good one, this is only because one thinks that there are good reasons *not* to bring an umbrella. One would not deny the hypothetical imperative because one is not rational, but because one thinks that there might be a more rationally acceptable hypothetical imperative to put in its place (e.g. 'If I want to stay dry, then I ought to wear a raincoat', or some such alternative). But when one thinks of such an alternative hypothetical imperative as better, one thinks that this replacement ought to be acknowledged by anyone as a better hypothetical imperative then the one regarding bringing an umbrella.

The general point is that, even if one thinks that morality is nothing but a set of hypothetical imperatives, one is nonetheless committed to the idea that if a reason for action is a *good* reason, it is a reason that is universally recognisable as such. If I think my hypothetical imperative is a good way of achieving my purpose, I think that every possible rational agent ought to be able to recognise that too. We might in fact think that just *what it is* for a reason to be a good reason is for me to think that no one would deny it. If someone did deny it, it must be either because they are mistaken or because I am mistaken about the matter.

Could one really believe that my reason for performing an action was a good reason, but that if someone disagreed with me, they would be correct *too*? Could it really be that I could be both correct and incorrect in thinking that an umbrella is a good way of keeping dry? One might say, 'well in some circumstances it is a good way, e.g. in a light shower, but in other circumstances, e.g. a storm, it is not'; here though it is really the case that we are talking about two different hypothetical imperatives ('if I want to keep dry in a light shower, then I ought to bring my umbrella' and 'if I want to keep dry in a storm, I ought to bring my umbrella'). The question is whether it is coherent to think that two people could be correct in thinking that a single hypothetical imperative gives an agent both a good reason and bad reason. Kant thinks (and he thinks any opponent must agree) that this is incoherent.

Thus I would suggest that in trying to motivate the idea of the power of the CI-test, Kant will be starting from commitments that he thinks any opponent must share, those of the authority of rationality and the universality of rationality. When Kant suggests that a 'formula' might be discovered from the 'mere concept of a categorical imperative' (4: 420), we can take him to be beginning from this starting point. If any agent is committed to these two claims about rationality, just by virtue of being a self-conscious rational agent who can adopt different hypothetical imperatives (and we all think that we are at least rational to this degree), then Kant thinks he can show that we are committed to *more* than this. We can, he thinks, focus just on those two commitments, to the authority and universality of rationality, and see that they *alone* – without any appeal to specific hypothetical imperatives – can provide us with a guide as to how we ought to act.

Kant thinks that by focusing on these commitments, we can make sense of there being two different questions that I can ask myself: firstly, I can ask myself 'what am I rationally committed to doing, given that I am a rational agent and that I have this desire?' but also the simpler question 'what am I rationally committed to doing (or not doing), given just that I am a rational agent?' We can see the outlines of Kant's strategy now – he has observed that one way to identify a genuinely moral principle is that it does not involve asking what it is good *for*, but is just when we recognise that something is a *good in itself*. Now Kant is suggesting that we can devise courses of action based on what is rationally required *for* realising this or that desire, but also based on what is *rational in itself*. The move that Kant is making is to say that moral actions are those that we recognise as demanded just by recognising that they are rational in themselves.

Kant is therefore drawing an extremely close connection between the moral and the rational. Does this then make him a moral rationalist? As a very rough definition, we might think of a rationalist as one who holds that our rational faculties could themselves uncover and justify specific truths that our non-rational capacities could not. Natural Law theorists (such as Aquinas for example) are arguably thought to have held that we could use our rational faculties to see what moral truths are contained therein. Such a theorist often held that our rational faculties are themselves guaranteed by God to be reliable, so that we could then use reason both to discover and to justify moral truths.

It is important to note though that Kant's rationalism will not be of this kind. Kant does share with the Natural Law theorists the belief that the moral and the rational are intimately connected. However, he does not hold the further rationalist claim that we are able to engage in some simple act of introspection (such as Descartes' method of meditation, for example), and just *see* what is contained within that rational faculty. Kant's conception of reason is not that of a storeroom of rational truths. We will not discover new moral truths in this way, Kant thinks; instead, he holds that our rational capacity, while it does not itself contain moral truths, can be used as a test or a procedure for seeing whether some maxim that we already possess is in fact a rationally and morally justified truth. To use a different metaphor, one should not think of our rational faculty as a kind of database containing a list of moral truths but instead as a kind of software testing program, whereby one can input a maxim at one end and receive as output at the other end a verdict as to whether that maxim is morally acceptable. Sometimes Kant's approach is called a kind of *rational proceduralism* in order to make distinct this difference between his approach and that of other moral rationalists.

As we have seen, Kant suggests that reflecting just on the very concept of a moral law or categorical imperative we can identify a formulation of the supreme moral principle. Kant in fact maintains that the supreme principle of morality can be given in several different formulations. He holds that all of these formulations are in one sense equivalent, while in another sense they are each supposed to reveal importantly different aspects of the supreme principle of morality. It is a matter of some controversy as to how Kant can maintain that all the formulations are distinct in one sense yet equivalent in another. There is a temptation also to think that there might be a single pre-eminent formulation that counts as the 'real' or 'fundamental' formulation. If that were the case, then the other formulations would be merely derivations or sub-formulations of that fundamental formulation. However, if this were a correct interpretation (and it is not obvious that it is), it is unclear as to *which* formulation is to be identified as the fundamental one.

The first formulation is commonly referred to as the *universal law formulation* (**FUL**):

There is therefore only a single categorical imperative, and it is this: *act only according to that maxim through which you can at the same time will that it become a universal law.* (4: 421)

Despite having just said that this is the 'only' categorical imperative, Kant immediately offers a reformulation of **FUL**, which is known as the *universal law of nature formulation* (**FULN**):

[S]*o act as if the maxim of your action were to become by your will a* **universal law of nature**. (4: 421)

Kant does not mean by this formulation that we will that our maxim become a natural law such as gravity (i.e. a law which we cannot help but obey), but rather that we are willing that our maxim be adopted as universally such that it is always voluntarily followed (i.e. so that it is as commonly followed a phenomenon as a law such as gravity or causation, etc.). It is unclear just how **FUL** and **FULN** are supposed to differ, or what extra point is being made when Kant gives us the formulation as **FULN** (as we shall see, he will presently offer two more formulations of the moral law, yet later on refer to having offered only three, suggesting that he perhaps did not see **FUL** and **FULN** as significantly different).

Kant now proceeds to offer a series of famous examples that demonstrate how the CI-test can be used in practice to decide whether or not something is a moral law. In each case, an imagined agent is in a particular situation where they are considering whether a certain course of action is morally acceptable or not. In each case, the imagined subject puts their maxim through the CI-test and in each case it fails. From this result they can infer that the course of action was not permissible and that a rule concerning its converse can be inferred. (For example, the first example concerns someone considering whether suicide is permissible. Their maxim fails the CI-test, from which one can infer that suicide is impermissible or that one must always respect one's life.)

This is what Kant means when he talks about proceeding just through consideration of the *form* of the moral law. The distinction that Kant is using here is the Aristotelian distinction between form and matter that we saw before. We do not, Kant thinks, have access to the matter of the moral law. This would be possible if we were the kind of creatures that could just identify, through pure reason or some other capacity, the specific list of things that are morally good or not ('*x* is good, *y*, is good, *z* is bad', etc.). It is just our fate that we do not have these kinds of intellectual powers, whereby we might just be able to 'see' rationally the fact that false promising (for instance) is morally wrong. Instead we have to try and figure out whether or not false promising is right or wrong by putting it through a more elaborate procedure. The form of universality is the mark of morality, as we have seen, so the procedure is one that tries to test a candidate maxim's moral status by appealing to considerations of its possible universalisation.

Kant seems to think that one frequently knows immediately when one has done something wrong – he earlier seemed to indicate that in most cases what he calls 'common human judging' (4: 412) is quite adequate for our needs with regard to figuring out what is the right and what is the wrong thing to do. But this effect is just one of good judgement, and it does not help us at all in answering the question: *why* is it that the thing that you can immediately recognise as morally wrong *is* morally wrong? It does not help much just to say 'well, because I just *see* that it's wrong'. Even though this is a common feature of our individual experiences, we would not want to take this as a standard account for identifying value in general – i.e. to say that '*x* is morally valuable if an agent sees *x* as morally valuable'. Apart from the fact that is does not explain anything about *what it is* that the agent is seeing as valuable, it is a hopelessly vague and general criterion to use, one that is open to abuse in obvious ways.

So instead Kant thinks that one can appeal to the *form* of the moral law, the feature of universality, and he devises a test using nothing but the idea that one's maxims ought to be universal in order to see if one can gain guidance from that alone. The fact that we are merely appealing to the form of the moral law does not mean that our reflections do not have any content, though. On the contrary, as we shall see, it is the very content of certain concepts, such as the meaning of the concepts like 'promising', that play an essential role when we try to develop universal maxims involving those concepts.

Before considering each of Kant's examples, a first thing to note is that Kant clearly meant for this test to be one that is used not in the idle consideration of some abstract question ('is lying wrong?', etc.) but rather when people find themselves in a particular situation where the moral acceptability of a specific course of action is in question ('is it acceptable in this situation for me to lie?'). What is more, Kant often seems to ascribe to his imagined subjects a standing moral belief that in usual circumstances something is in fact permissible or impermissible or obligatory – their only question is whether or not *this* particular case is one of those normal circumstances. Although it is somewhat unclear, it can look as if Kant is attributing to his subjects moral beliefs that are not in doubt for them at all (e.g. 'normally one shouldn't lie but is it acceptable in this situation for me to lie?'). Perhaps he thinks that we do not need to deploy any special philosophical machinery in order to figure out that normally one should not lie, but only need to do so in unusual or tricky cases (however, the reader should note that these are all controversial and difficult claims that are typical of the challenges one faces in attempting to provide an interpretation of Kant's approach).

There are several important distinctions that must be understood with regard to Kant's examples. The first distinction is between *duties to oneself* and *duties to others*. This distinction is clear enough. Kant uses the examples of suicide and the act of refraining from developing one's one natural talents as examples of duties that are primarily to oneself; as examples of duties to others, he discusses the cases of making a lying promise to someone in order to borrow money and of deciding not to help others in need when such an occasion arises. Since each maxim *fails* the CI-test, the inferred results are that respecting one's life, developing one's natural gifts, promising sincerely and helping others in need are all categorical imperatives.

A second distinction is between *perfect* and *imperfect* duties (4: 421). This distinction is less clear, though one initial characterisation that one could make follows from Kant's claim that a perfect duty is 'one that allows of no exception to the advantage of inclination' (4: 421, note). This is an initially confusing claim, since it implies that imperfect duties can allow exceptions when inclination pushes us another way, and this would seem to oppose everything Kant has said before about inclination and duty. However, a plausible way of understanding them is to note firstly that perfect duties refer to a particular type of action that is strictly either prohibited or demanded in all possible cases. For example, Kant holds that I can never, in any circumstances, perform the specific actions of committing suicide or of making a false promise.

His examples of imperfect duties – those of developing one's talents and helping others in need – are more vague action-types than the specific actions mentioned as perfect duties. There are many different ways in which one might develop one's talents or help others in need. Furthermore, it can be that in order to follow these action-types sometimes we might have to perform actions that look like they run against them. For example, if I were a talented doctor or professional golfer or some such, it might be that I have a duty not to neglect those gifts but to practise and develop them. It can often be the case, though, that I must not over-practise, that I must take breaks, and sometimes very extended ones, so that I do not burn out and can pursue my goals more effectively in the long run. In this way, if we think of imperfect duties as a kind of action that indicate a general policy for one's life, we can see that it is perfectly consistent that one might be engaged in different actions as a way of fulfilling that general policy. Someone might ask me whether I might not be neglecting my golfing talents in taking a year off to go backpacking, but it may well be the case that one has reasoned that this is in fact necessary for one's overall pursuit of that exact general policy.

This is perhaps more compelling still in considering the imperfect duty to help others in need. It would be a severe moral system indeed that demanded that one could never adopt a short-term policy of not helping those in need. It is surely the case that there is nothing wrong in people pursuing their own ends and following their own inclinations and desires on occasion. All Kant means when he says that helping others in need is an imperfect duty is that we must live our lives under this general policy, and that we cannot live our lives under a general policy of living one's life solely in the pursuit of one's own desired ends. This contrasts sharply with perfect duties – here there is no wriggle room as to how we implement the policy, since the policy refers to a very specific action-type. One can *never* make a false promise, not even as a means to some further virtuous end. Similarly, one can never commit suicide, even if one has some reasoning pattern whereby in a bigger picture it is morally acceptable to do so.

Thus from Kant's first two distinctions we can make out the duties shown in Table 1:

Table 1

Type of duty	*To oneself*	*To others*
Perfect	Suicide	False promises
Imperfect	Neglecting talents	Non-assistance

The distinction between perfect and imperfect duties corresponds to a third and final distinction, that between the two *stages* of the CI-test. The test is supposed to proceed through an initial formulation of some maxim indicating a desired course of action. Next, one puts that maxim through a process of universalisation, whereby one imagines a world wherein everyone always acts in accordance with that maxim. In some cases, Kant holds, we can see straightaway that the maxim is incoherent in that imagined world. If the CI-test produces that result, then we know that we have identified the opposed course of action as a perfect duty. This part of the CI-test is often referred to as the *contradiction in conception* test, since Kant claims that when a maxim fails at this first stage it is because that 'maxim cannot even be *thought* without contradiction as a law of nature' (4: 424).

Some maxims, however, can pass the contradiction in conception test but nevertheless fail at a second stage. It might be, Kant claims, that we can conceive of a maxim in its universalised form but that we cannot subsequently *will* that it become a universal law. This second stage of the CI-test is known as the *contradiction in the will* test. Kant argues that the maxims of neglecting one's talents and refraining from helping those in need are conceivable in their universal form (i.e. we can imagine a world where everyone adopted and lived by those maxims) but we cannot will that such a world be the case.

The notion of what it is to will, or to be unable to will, that something be a universal law is left unclear in Kant's writing. On the one hand it seems to be something weaker than the strict logical contradiction, e.g. the assertion that both p and not p, that Kant seems to be appealing to in his characterisation of the first stage of the test. On the other hand, it seems that Kant needs it to be stronger than merely *wishing* that a maxim be a universal law, since wishing it to be so would be merely a statement of wanting it to be so or liking if it were so, and Kant is clear that at no stage of the CI-test is any work done by appeal to inclinations – it is still supposed to be a purely *rational* test, even at the second step of identifying contradictions.

Perhaps one way of thinking of the notion of being incapable to will that something is a universal law is in terms of rational *incoherence* rather than strict logical contradiction. To use an analogy from epistemology, it is notable that what is referred to as 'Moore's paradox' is not in fact a strict logical paradox. Moore's paradox concerns the imagined example of a subject making the following assertion: 'It is raining but I do not believe that it is.' There is definitely something strange about someone who would make an assertion like this, but the strangeness is not that she would have said something logically contradictory. The assertion is made up of two distinct propositions – 'it is raining' and 'I don't believe it is raining'. If we consider these two in isolation there is nothing logically contradictory about them – it is certainly logically possible that I might believe that something is the case while in fact it is not the case.

Instead the strangeness comes from the situation whereby someone might combine both these propositions in a single sentence and perform the action of asserting that whole sentence. Although there is not a logical contradiction there is perhaps what is sometimes called a performative contradiction: in asserting 'it is raining but I don't believe that it is' I have committed myself to the truth of something in the first part of the sentence and withdrawn that commitment in the second part of the sentence. I have not committed a logical fallacy but I have perhaps incurred some kind of rational incoherence in terms of my commitments as to what is the case. Perhaps in the case of imperfect duties, with maxims that fail the second step of the CI-test, we can consider the failure to be related to the failure incurred by the subject of Moore's paradox. It is not that the maxim is logically self-contradictory but rather that I cannot commit myself to the thought that it be adopted by all possible agents without incurring some kind of rational incoherence in how that maxim relates to my other commitments.

We will return to this topic presently, but before we do so, it is worth examining in general what might be going on at the *first* step of the CI-test, where some maxims fail just in the act of thinking of them as universal laws. (It should be noted that in what follows I will present just one kind of interpretation of Kant's CI-test, but there are many others, and too many to survey in this book. Many of the difficulties in interpreting the CI-test concern how to understand what exactly is going on when one is imagining a world where the candidate maxim has been universalised. Some prefer what is called a 'logical reading' – here the failure to universalise is brought about because some kind of strict logical contradiction has been realised. Other readings include 'practical' and 'teleological' readings, which claim that the stages of the CI-test should not be understood in terms of strict logical contradiction but rather in terms of overall rational coherence in the adoption of one's practical goals or aims. In what follows I will present a more 'logical' interpretation of the CI-test, though the reader should be aware that there are other competing readings to be explored.)

It might be helpful in approaching Kant's daunting apparatus to consider first a non-philosophical case from ordinary life, in order to understand the general style of thinking that the CI-test might involve. There is a phenomenon frequently reported in the media called 'Nimbyism'. 'Nimby' stands for 'not in my back yard', and is usually intended as a somewhat pejorative term for someone who opposes national political policies being implemented in their own local area. One might note first of all that there is nothing at all wrong with objecting to some policy being enacted that will damage or otherwise harm one's own area. So why then is it considered a bad thing to be a Nimby? The term is used because sometimes objections to potentially harmful changes in one's own local area can reflect a certain kind of hypocrisy, one that might even indicate a kind of irrationality. The hypocrisy arises if a person is on one the hand *in favour* of a policy at the state level (imagine, for example, that it is a policy suggesting the need to build more prisons nationally) but the person *also* opposes the implementation of that policy in their own local area ('no prisons in my neighbourhood!'). So the Nimby holds something like

(1) φ ought to be implemented in the state (except in area *k*)

where φ stands for the policy, and *k* stands for a local area. So far there is nothing inconsistent, irrational or hypocritical about holding (1) as it is formulated: it might be correct to think that, although the policy ought to be implemented for the benefit of the state as a whole, there is some *particular* reason for thinking that it should not be implemented in area *k*. So let us assume that our Nimby has some reason, **R**, for this idea:

(1*) φ ought to be implemented in the state (except in area *k* on the grounds that **R**)

The accusation of Nimbyism depends on the nature of reason **R**. The reason for the policy not being implemented in area *k* has to be *special*, such that it suggests that although the policy is fine for everyone else, there are special reasons why it should not be implemented in area *k* in particular. Perhaps on occasion someone does have such reasons, but someone is accused of being a Nimby when it is thought that **R** *does not* constitute a special reason for making an exception of *k*.

Why would it be a problem if **R** does not constitute a special reason for making an exception of *k*? If this were the case, it might be that *anyone* could claim that **R** gives them *just as good* a reason for claiming that the policy should not be implemented in *their* area either. We can see a kind of logical inconsistency in our Nimby's reasoning if we follow the thinking along, because it seems that the Nimby must hold that all of the following are true:

(1*) φ ought to be implemented in the state (except in area *k* on the grounds that **R**)
(2) **R** holds equally well for any other of the given areas (*l, m, n, o, p* . . . etc.) of the state.
Therefore,
(3) For any given area of the state (*l, m, n, o, p* . . . etc.), φ ought to be implemented, except in the given areas *l, m, n, o, p* . . . etc.

We can see that the Nimby holds: firstly, that the policy should be implemented nationally; secondly, that it should not be implemented in his local area for a reason that holds validly for that area; thirdly, that the reasoning works *just as well* to make an exception of *every* area of the nation. But in this case the reasoning follows that if there is a good reason for thinking that the policy should not be implemented in one area, there is a good reason for thinking that the policy should not be implemented in every area. Thus it seems that the Nimby thinks that the policy *should* be implemented in the state but that there are good rational grounds for claiming that it *should not* be implemented in any of the areas that go to make up the state! Therefore, the Nimby is committed to the idea that the policy both should and should not be implemented in the state. This is a kind of logical contradiction and the Nimby must give up his endorsement of (1*).

This example can perhaps shed some light about how Kant thinks that just by appealing to the authority and universality of reason we can sometimes see that certain courses of action commit one to a kind of contradiction. The kind of contradiction is one that we see brought about in a world where we have imagined that everyone has adopted or could adopt the same reason for his or her actions as we are considering for the justification of our maxim. As we saw with the discussion of the universality of rationality, if I think x is rational for me, then there must be a sense in which I can understand that x is rational for *any* agent.

It is important to point out first of all what universalisability is *not* – universalisability is not a process whereby one imagines that everyone has adopted a rule and then calculates what the *consequences* of that would be. Were Kant to do this, he would be falling back into a consequentialist way of looking at things, and we have seen from the first section that Kant is opposed to consequentialist reasoning as a means of moral evaluation. Instead, what Kant is suggesting is a process whereby one imagines that everyone has adopted a rule and then one imagines whether that society would be properly described as *rationally consistent or coherent* in the way they behave. Kant thinks that when we put some maxims to this test, we see that the society that we have imagined involves various kinds of rational breakdown.

As I have already suggested, Kant thinks that all these maxims have a certain structure. He thinks that they are all cases where an agent is seeking to justify their action by making an *exception* for their own particular circumstance. Kant claims more that this in fact, and that his analysis will reveal that when we are sometimes advocating a certain action to ourselves we are not in fact saying

> that our maxim should become a universal law, since that is impossible for us, but that its opposite should rather generally remain a law; we just take the liberty of making an *exception* to it for ourselves, or (just for this once) to the advantage of our inclination. (4: 424)

This is itself a controversial move, since it seems to commit Kant to thinking that these maxims can be analysed in these terms – however, for the purposes of this analysis we will grant him this thought. We can think of the maxims under consideration as being made up of two clauses. The first clause, which I will call the *norm clause*, states how things ought to be in normal or regular circumstances. The second clause, which I will call the *exception clause*, states the conditions when it is acceptable to deviate from those regular circumstances and to make an exception (recall the case of the Nimby, who held both a norm clause that the policy should be implemented nationally and an exception clause that an exception should be made of his own area).

Kant's first example is in the category of perfect duties to oneself, and concerns that of an agent considering the possibility of ending their life on the grounds that he judges that the future strongly suggests hardship (4: 421–2). Kant is clear that the reasoning that the agent is suggesting is whether in this particular circumstance it might be acceptable to end one's life:

> Now he tries out: whether the maxim of his action could possibly become a universal law of nature. But his maxim is: from self-love I make it my principle to shorten my life if, when protracted any longer, it threatens more ill than it promises agreeableness. (4: 422)

One of the most difficult tasks in interpreting Kant's examples is to identify exactly how the maxim under consideration should be formulated before one puts it through the CI-test. I am presenting an account where in each case an agent is considering whether in a certain particular circumstance one can deviate from one's normal course of behaviour. Here Kant holds that the subject is motivated by 'self-love', i.e. self-interest, to consider ending his life. The implication is that there is a normal circumstance where it is part of human nature's normal self-interested function to prolong one's life – he says that human beings' disposition to self-interest is a proper part of their nature, 'the function of which it is to impel towards the advancement of life'. The agent in this case is considering whether, despite this being the *normal* function of human beings' nature that we normally respect, there might be a case where we can disregard that normal function and make an exception. I would suggest then that the agent is considering the following maxim:

(*Suicide*) One ought to follow human nature's disposition to prolong life, except if one perceives an advantage (in avoiding ill) by ending it.

Now Kant suggests that if we submit this maxim to the CI-test, we can immediately see that it fails at the first stage, in that we cannot even conceive clearly of a world where this maxim was adopted universally. Why is this world conceptually incoherent? My suggestion is that there is a sense in which in that imagined world we lose a grip on the meaning of one of the concepts involved in the maxim. The question is: can we still make sense of the idea that human nature's proper function is to *prolong* life if we imagine that everyone's nature now allows them to end it on *any* occasion? One way of thinking of the function of self-interest is that it is a function that stirs the agent to prolong their life in the hope of gaining some future benefit for themselves. But then one might think that the purpose of self-interest as a means of prolonging life is that it can motivate the agent to keep going in the face of temporary hardship. The thought then is that, *even if* the agent perceives the risk of some future disadvantage to himself, the function of self-interest will keep him in the pursuit of life in the face of that risk.

If this is the case though, then we can see that a strange result emerges in the imagined world where everyone holds the (*Suicide*) maxim. In this world anyone can chose to shorten their lives *whenever* they perceive that there might be some future ill avoided by doing so. But in this world then it is simply not the case that human nature's inherent instinct is to prolong its life in the face of challenges, since in this world it is in human beings' nature to offer themselves the option of ending their life on any occasion whatsoever in which they perceive a challenge. In the imagined world that the agent is considering, he is claiming that it is *both* in human beings' nature to prolong their life in the face of challenges (as stated in the norm clause: 'one ought to follow human nature's disposition to prolong life) *and* that it is in human beings' nature to end their life in the face of any challenge (as stated in the exception clause: 'except if one perceives an advantage (in avoiding ill) by ending it').

The result is that in this world we do not even have a concept of human nature's normal disposition for prolonging life at all anymore, so cannot coherently imagine any maxim involving that concept. Thus the (*Suicide*) maxim fails the first contradiction in conception test:

But then one soon sees that a nature whose law it were to destroy itself by means of the same sensation the function of which it is to impel towards the advancement of life, would contradict itself and would thus not subsist as a nature, hence that that maxim could not possibly take the place of a universal law of nature, and consequently conflicts entirely with the supreme principle of all duty. (4: 422)

The conclusion is that one is never permitted to shorten one's life on the grounds of avoiding disadvantage, and so one must always respect one's own life in the face of such temptations.

We can perhaps see Kant's strategy most clearly by looking in detail at his second example, that of the prohibition upon making a false promise (a perfect duty to others). When one states to oneself 'I'll take Richard's money, but I don't really think I'll be in a position to pay it back easily by the time we've agreed', one is in fact implicitly endorsing for oneself a more general maxim (call it the *False Promises* maxim) with the following structure:

(*False Promises*) One ought not make false promises, except when to do so would avoid a difficulty.

Here the difficulty being avoided is that, were one to tell Richard the truth, and say that one does not expect to be in a position to pay him back, he might not give the loan at all.

It is certainly the case that Richard and you are only interacting upon the assumption that you both sincerely endorse the idea that one ought not make false promises – there is a standing assumption of sincerity by both parties in order for any arrangement of this kind to take place. However, I take it that Kant's point here is far stronger – he is claiming that when one is justifying one's own behaviour to oneself (unbeknownst to Richard) one is in fact endorsing the idea that *in general*, one ought not to make false promises, but adding on a proviso that, despite this being a good rule in general, there are cases where it does not apply, and that *this* instance is one of those cases. If we look above we see that the false promises maxim is phrased as an endorsement of the norm clause ('one ought not make false promises') while also endorsing what is expressed in the exception clause, the idea of there being a special circumstance that constitutes an exception to the norm ('except when to do so would avoid a difficulty').

Is this plausible? When I falsely promise to pay back Tom's money, am I really endorsing a claim that a rule should hold normally but just not in *this* case? Well, we might ask the following question – if one takes oneself to be morally justified in making a lying promise here, just what form would the rule take? One might take oneself to be endorsing the claim that one ought always to make false promises whenever one wishes. But surely this is not correct. In endorsing (*False Promises*) above I am taking myself to be justified only in *this* exceptional case. I do not take myself to be part of that crowd that expresses whatever lie they think will get them whatever they happen to want at the time. One is not claiming that there is no moral difference between promising truly and promising falsely or that the issue of lying to get what you want is not a moral issue. The person who promises falsely is not a moral nihilist – they do not think that there is no such thing as the right or the wrong thing to do here – rather they are claiming that the issue *is* a moral one, and the correct attitude to take is that there are certain cases where it is morally acceptable to make a false promise.

I take Kant to be making a plausible psychological claim here, which is that when we are justifying to ourselves a certain type of action, our justification story can often take on a what we might think of as a kind of '*yeah, but*' structure. If someone, hearing that we have done something that would normally be considered wrong, challenges us about it, our justification takes the form of a defence:

'yeah, normally I wouldn't have done that, but on this occasion . . .'. One says to one's challenger: 'Of course I endorse the general rule of action that you endorse, but think there are sometimes circumstances where it is acceptable to deviate from the rule, such as . . . etc.' We hear this kind of challenge and response all the time, though it is usually implied in our ordinary conversation:

'Didn't you tell your mother that you were going to visit her on Saturday?'
'Yeah, but I came down with the flu.'

Or,

'Didn't you tell your mother that you were going to visit her on Saturday?'
'Yeah, but I preferred to stay in and watch the *Sopranos* marathon.'

Notice the difference in these cases. In both questions, there is the assumption that one normally ought to visit one's mother. The first response states that, while one ought to have visited one's mother, in this circumstance sickness made it impossible to do so. Here we would take this as a valid excuse. In the second response though, we would be rather generous to the person to think that the TV show marathon constituted a factor that made it impossible for them to visit their mother. Instead it is more natural to take it that they are saying that their preference for staying in *justified* their not going to visit their mother.

In order to see how the CI-test might handle a case like this, we must first consider what it is that we understand by the concept of 'promising'. Analysing the nature of promising is a philosophical task in itself, but for our purposes we can just note that there is a difference between expressing to someone one's *intention* to perform a certain action ('I'm going to go to the party this Saturday') and *promising to that someone* that you will do that action ('I promise you that I'm going to go to the party this Saturday'). When one promises someone that one is going to go to a party, the *promisor* (the person making the promise) is saying to the *promisee* (the person to whom the promise is made) that they can *rely* upon our performing that action – the promisor is making a kind of commitment to the promisee. When one promises something one is saying *both* that the one intends to do that thing *and* that the other person can rely upon us to do it (i.e. the promisee can plan and co-ordinate *their* future actions along the assumption that we will be performing that action).

We can see this by imagining what would be the consequences if we ended up not going to the party. If we had merely expressed to someone an intention to go to the party, it would be perfectly appropriate to justify one's not going by saying 'oh, I changed my mind. I decided I'd prefer to stay in and watch TV'. But imagine that we had *promised* to someone that we would go to the party. It is no excuse then to say in that case that we merely changed our mind because we had a change in our preferences. The person might reasonably complain that when we promise someone that we will do something, what we mean is that we will do it *even if* we have a change of preference in the meantime. They might complain that when we realised that our preferences had changed and that we would rather stay in, we should have reasoned 'oh, I don't really want to go to the party anymore, but I promised that I would, so I will'. We can see then that one of the features of the very *concept* of promising is that it involves something like the sincere expression of an intention to follow through on a course of action irrespective of one's possible later changing desires regarding that course of action. Although this is a slightly abstract way of putting it, it is something that we all intuitively understand to be involved with the concept of promising.

With this idea in mind, we can reconstruct a possible reading of why Kant thinks the CI-procedure shows that we must always keep our promises. The question we must ask ourselves, he thinks, is whether it is possible to universalise the maxim that it is acceptable to makes a false promise whenever one perceives that it would be advantageous to do so. Keeping with the analysis suggested above, we might imagine that the formula would have to be phrased in terms of a norm clause and an exception clause. We begin with a situation whereby one is considering whether it is morally acceptable for one to make a lying promise in this case. I might try and justify it to myself with the following general rule (which is an equivalent expression of the version given above):

(*False Promises*) One should always make one's promises sincerely, except when one judges that it would be to one's advantage not to do so.

Now we attempt to run that maxim through the CI-procedure, by imagining a world whereby *everyone* endorsed that maxim. Does the maxim make sense when universalised like this? One might say at first glance that it does – there is nothing immediately incoherent in this formulation. Consider though the meaning of the concept of promising that was discussed above. It is not just that when we imagine this possible world we are imagining a world where, when one indicates that one is making a promise to someone, the promisee can never tell whether or not the promise made is a sincere or a lying one (that is the case in *this* world!). Rather, it is that in the imagined world the promisee *never* takes the promisor's act of expressing a promise to actually entail that she has in fact made *any kind* of commitment to act in a certain way, since the act of expressing a promise is compatible with the possibility that no real promise has been made, because in this imagined world making a false promise, i.e. a promise to perform actions to which you are not in fact committed, is just normal practice.

But now it seems that in this world we are losing our grip on the notion of promising altogether. Imagine someone asking whether another individual intends to perform an action. The response comes 'yes, she expressed to me her intention to do that'. Imagine that then the person asks whether we are *sure* that she will do it. In this world responding 'well, she has promised to me that she will do it' means nothing, because in this world, where false promises are normal practice, saying that 'I promise to do *x*' does not offer any greater commitment than saying 'I intend to do *x*'. But the basic notion of promising with which we started was just that it *does* involve more than merely expressing one's intention to perform an action.

Thus in the world imagined by the first step of the CI-test the concept of promising has lost the particular conceptual content that makes it a distinct concept in the first place. In willing (*False Promises*), Kant says, I am committed to a possible world in which *both* (a) I can make a false promise (and so where there have to be promisees and promisors, i.e. agents who understand the distinct concept of promising) *and* (b) there is no distinct concept of promising. If this is the universalised maxim regarding false promising, then we can see why Kant would think that it involves a kind of rational self-contradiction.

If everyone thought that this maxim was acceptable, then we really would not think there was any *difference* between someone promising us something and someone merely stating their intention to do something. Thus there is a kind of logical contradiction that can be revealed just by examining the rational implications of one's maxim. I cannot conceive of a world where I can both promise (sincerely or insincerely) to do something but where promising itself as a distinct practice does not exist. (Again, readers should be aware that this is just one among many possible readings of how Kant's method is supposed to work; for example, a 'practical reading' of the CI-test explains the false promising maxim as failing because in universalising the maxim an agent is both willing an end – getting a loan, for example – but also willing that conditions obtain that deny her the practical means to realise that end – i.e. there being people who are disposed to believe a promise to pay back a loan – and in that way a kind of practical contradiction is incurred. Readers can determine for themselves which of the interpretations better suit Kant's overall strategy here.)

In putting the false promising maxim though the CI-test, we come to see that it fails the test, and that we cannot adopt it as a rule to guide our behaviour. In fact we can derive the converse rule to guide our behaviour ('never make false promises → always promise sincerely', etc.). But we have not arrived at this point by virtue of any kind of super intellectual power that allows us to 'see' the goodness of promising truthfully. We did not get here because we have access to the *matter* of the moral law. Instead we simply tried to appeal to the rational *form* of the moral law – the idea that, if anything is moral, then it is something that should hold equally and universally for all. Just by appealing to the form of the moral law, Kant thinks that we are able to devise a test that functions as the best moral methodology one can have.

The third example, that of an imperfect duty to oneself, concerns an agent who is considering the possibility of not developing their natural abilities, and instead devoting their life to idleness and pleasure. The agent now wonders whether this general policy for living his life is morally acceptable and 'whether his maxim of neglecting his natural gifts, besides its agreement with his propensity to amusement, also agrees with what one calls duty' (4: 423). The maxim I would suggest the agent is considering is as follows:

(*Neglecting Talents*) One ought to develop one's natural gifts, except when one perceives an advantage in neglecting them for the sake of pleasure.

Again, I would suggest that Kant sees the agent in question as grasping that in the normal run of things, developing one's talents can bring one all kinds of advantages, including many particular occasions of advantage that one cannot foresee. The agent is considering whether, *despite this*, there might be more advantage to be had in neglecting those talents and maximising one's idle enjoyment instead. Kant concedes that in this case, the maxim does pass the first step of the CI-test: we could imagine, he thinks, a world where every agent held this maxim without us thereby losing grasp of the very concept of developing one's talents. Perhaps this is due to the fact that 'development of talents' is a much more vague concept than the concepts of 'suicide' or 'promising'. As I suggested before, one can develop one's talents in many different ways on particular occasions (for example by taking time off, etc.), and perhaps then the concept lacks the specificity required to generate a strict logical contradiction.

As such, Kant now considers whether (*Neglecting Talents*) might pass the second stage of the CI-test, the contradiction in the will test. Here he says that we can see that the maxim fails, since 'as a rational being he necessarily wills that all capacities in him be developed, because they serve him and are given to him for all sorts of possible purposes' (4: 423). It is not clear exactly how this failure has arisen. A difficulty is to see how the reasoning here is different from the prudential reasoning that Kant opposes. It certainly looks like the agent here is making a calculation of what it would be prudent for him to do with regard to realising his ends, yet we know that this cannot be Kant's meaning here.

One possible reading is as follows: in imagining a world where everyone at any time can opt to neglect their own talents whenever they perceive an advantage in doing so, then we would have willed a world where talents would in fact go undeveloped, since developing talents is at least sometimes bothersome, and thus everyone would at some point inevitably see some advantage in not doing so. Now though the thought is that the agent has willed a world where he himself does not have the possible means available to him to pursue even his life of enjoyment. Since the pursuit of enjoyment is itself a vague concept reflecting a general policy, there are many ways of pursuing that end, and the agent himself might need to fall back on some of his own talents (and perhaps the talents of others) on particular occasions in order to achieve this general policy. Therefore there is a kind of rational incoherence that the agent endorsing (*Neglecting Talents*) encounters, which is that even in order to pursue the general policy expressed in the exception clause, the agent must *also* pursue the general policy expressed in the norm clause. While these general policies are not logically contradictory (since they are too vague for us to say exactly how they would contradict each other in practice), they are nevertheless clearly rationally incompatible long-term policy commitments. Thus this maxim too must be rejected and the general policy expressed in the norm clause, that of developing one's talents, must be adopted.

As an example of an imperfect duty towards others, Kant finally considers the example of an agent who is considering a radical policy change in their lifestyle. In effect they are considering whether, although people should normally help each other when one of them is in need and the other is in a position to offer assistance, it is acceptable that someone might adopt a policy of complete independence from others. The person is considering whether it is morally acceptable that an agent might choose to live their life on the basis of a calculation that in the long run, they will be better off without being either the donor or the beneficiary in these kinds of social interactions. That is, they consider the possibility of living independently of both the practices of helping or being helped, without either giving or accepting aid from any other agent (4: 423). The maxim here might be as follows:

(*Non-Assistance*) One ought to help others in need, unless I perceive an advantage in the policy of living independently from the practice of giving aid.

Here again Kant says that this maxim is in fact conceptually coherent when universalised, i.e. it passes the first stage of the CI-test. Thus Kant thinks there is no logical contradiction in there being a world where (*Non-Assistance*) is universally held. However, Kant now claims that although conceiving of this world is possible (the very concept of aiding others has not disappeared in this imagined world), it is nevertheless the case that (*Non-Assistance*) is still rationally unacceptable. The maxim passes the contradiction is conception test but fails the contradiction in will test. Kant puts it as follows:

But even though it is possible that a universal law of nature could very well subsist according to that maxim, it is still impossible to **will** that such a principle hold everywhere as a law of nature. For a will that resolved upon this would conflict with itself, as many cases can yet come to pass in which one needs the love and compassion of others, and in which, by such a law of nature sprung from his own will, he would rob himself of all hope of the assistance he wishes for himself. (4: 423)

The argument here is again very obscure and one has to be cautious in its interpretation. Firstly, we can see that Kant seems again to phrase things in a curiously consequentialist way, whereby the problem is supposed to be that in this imagined world there would be negative consequences for the individual. As before though, this cannot be Kant's reasoning, since it reduces the CI-test to a piece of elaborate prudential reasoning. Secondly, there is the already mentioned obscurity of the notion of willing. It is not clear as to just what it is to be unable to will this maxim, despite being able to conceive of it clearly – Kant claims there is 'conflict' within one's own rational will even if that conflict is not one of straight-out self-contradiction. It is difficult, though, to see how this 'conflict' is supposed to make it *impossible* to will the maxim as a universal law.

One possible interpretation is that by 'willing' here Kant means something like *rationally endorsing* or *rationally committing* to a plan of action. It might be, as we saw with Moore's paradox, that I can conceive of an endorsement which is logically coherent in one sense but which is nevertheless not coherent with regard to the performance of rationally committing to that policy. Perhaps then Kant is saying that while it is logically possible that we can imagine a world where everyone endorsed the maxim, we cannot imagine that in that world they would be living lives that are coherent in terms of their capacity for practical rationality more generally.

It is still unclear why this must be the case, however, even on this reading. Kant seems to indicate that the source of the conflict is that the agent considering the maxim cannot rule out the possibility that they will be in need of assistance at some future point. Of course, the agent might accept that claim, but just re-assert that nevertheless they are willing to forego the assistance they might need in the future. The whole point of considering the maxim was to consider a life that might not be easier even taking into account that one would not be able to benefit from the assistance of others.

Perhaps though Kant's point here is that it is hard to imagine what a world where everyone adopted this maxim would be like in terms of the rational commitments and coherence of its agents. For example, there is a question as to whether the imagined world would even count as a *community* of agents at all in this case. We might think that part of what makes up the concept of a community is more than merely a collection of agents but of a collection of agents who take themselves to be connected through their interactions. Furthermore, one of the universal truths about human agents is their *finitude* – they are not limitless in their powers or abilities. So one might think that part of just what it is to be a member of a community is to be part of a collection of agents who can *rely* on each other in reaction to the condition of their individual finitude – in other words, to be a member of a community is to view oneself as a member of a collection of agents that are at least capable of helping each other out.

If this is the case (and it is only one possible reading of Kant's strategy here) then there *is* something practically incoherent in imagining oneself both as a member of a community and as someone endorsing the maxim to live independently of the practice of giving aid. If we universalise that maxim and imagine a world where everyone adopted that same course of action, we would have imagined something where the universal practice of living independently is conceivable, but only at the cost of no longer having a grip on how that the agents in that world constitute a community of rational agents. The agent considering (*Non-Assistance*) was not considering opting out of a community altogether, rather he was only considering opting out of a particular practice within that community, namely the practice of giving and receiving aid when it is needed. The maxim fails at the second step because the agent generates a contradiction in his will, in that he cannot coherently endorse both the practice of being a member of a community and that of living independently of aid at the same time.

Kant's examples of **FUL** and **FULN** in action are themselves controversial and difficult to interpret, and scores of philosophers since have wondered whether the test can be extended to every possible morally relevant case, or whether counterexamples can be produced. To evaluate this question though is beyond the scope of this book – for present purposes we can see the general tenor of Kant's approach, which is the appeal to features of rationality itself as an actual source of instruction about what we ought to do in particular cases of moral indecision. Kant did not think that the CI-test or the *Groundwork* itself was a complete account of what is involved in living a moral life, though he did think that it was an essential part of that story.

Kant continues his analysis with the claim that his methodology has been entirely opposed to an empirical one and has instead proceeded not by any empirical claims about human beings but just by consideration of 'the concept of the will of a rational being as such' (4: 426). He returns here to a claim that we have seen already, namely that such a will 'is thought as a capacity to determine itself to action *in conformity with the representation of certain laws*' (4: 427). While we act in conformity with laws of nature, such as cause and effect, we also can understand ourselves as creatures that can act in conformity with what we self-consciously identify *as* a law, even if it does not impose itself physically upon us. Our nature as both physical and self-conscious agents allows us to describe ourselves in accordance with two very different descriptions that explain our actions.

Imagine that you witness one person slapping another, and you ask a third person why they think that person did what they did. It would be a strange answer if they were to say 'well, certain neurons fired in his brain which sent signals to his nerve endings, which in turn stimulated his muscles and which then generated motion in his hand such that it made contact with the other person's face'. This description of their action is perfectly normal insofar as it aspires to give an account of the chain of physical causes that brought about the action. But the response would still be a strange one, since what we normally mean when we ask 'why did that happen?' is not 'what are the relevant laws of nature that were in operation here?' but rather 'what was their *reason* for performing that action?' In fact we intuitively take it that one might give a complete and exhaustive story of the physical causal processes that underlie the action without even *asking*, let alone answering, the question regarding the reason why someone performed that action.

Thus we naturally take there to be two distinct domains for the explanation of action, the physical and the rational. Kant has two important claims here: firstly, he is claiming that human beings are peculiar in that we can and must see ourselves as beings who occupy both domains coterminously; secondly, we see each domain as governed by laws that each carry a kind of necessity. We can ask a person 'did he *have* to do that?' As before, we can understand this question in relation to either the physical or the rational domains of explanation. We might be asking the question (though it would be a strange philosophical reaction to the scene) whether the physical causal events were necessitated by laws of nature and the general principle of cause and effect, i.e. we might have meant by the question 'was there a deterministic causal chain that led to that event?'

More often, though, when we ask whether someone *had* to do some action, we are asking whether it was *rationally required* of them to perform that act. Someone might answer that they *did* have to slap the other person, say in order to prevent them from committing a terrible crime. Here they would be appealing to your sense of instrumental reason (it was a good strategy for achieving their end) but also to your sense of one's having to obey a necessary demand set by a normative standard. They might say 'I could not allow that person to commit that terrible crime, so I had to slap them in order to prevent that happening'. When they say that they 'could not allow' the event to happen, they are saying that there was a moral necessity that imposed a rational norm or standard upon them.

The norm, though not itself a law of nature, is similar to a law of nature in that it sets out what must happen within a certain domain of explanation – in this case the domain of rational moral action. An obvious difference, one that Kant repeatedly points out, is that while a physical law of nature stipulates what *must* and so in fact *does* always happen, a law of reason stipulates what *must* happen (in the sense of a moral 'must') but *does not* in fact always happen. In Kant's terminology, we would say that with regard to the will's action, it can act in accordance not with physical laws, but with laws it *represents* to itself as holding within the rational domain. Just because we are self-conscious agents capable of acting freely and for reasons, we are agents who can represent to ourselves things that we take it that we and any rational agent *must* do.

Kant distinguishes between different types of ground of the will's 'self-determination' (4: 427), by which he means something like the basis of that which moves us to act. These bases are goal-directed: they indicate some achievement or 'end' towards which the action is targeted. On the one hand, we can have ends that are based on our desires, which Kant calls *subjective ends*; on the other we can have ends that are based upon our moral reasons, which are called *objective ends* (since they hold for every possible agent, unlike subjective ends, which are conditional on an agent having the relevant desires). If we are motivated to a subjective end, Kant says that we have an *incentive*; if we have an objective end, we have a *motive*. Clearly, this is not our common understanding of these words – some might think that 'incentive' and 'motive' are largely interchangeable in our ordinary use – and so we will have to recall that Kant is using these words in a restricted technical sense.

Kant is attempting to link up several different concepts together, for example desire with hypothetical imperatives and 'material' principles (i.e. principles that are directed towards some particular subject matter). We can get a sense of the divisions and groupings from Table 2:

Table 2

Ground of the will's self-determination	Desire	Reason
Type of end	Subjective	Objective
Type of basis of action	Incentive	Motive
Relation to the agent	Relative	Universal
Type of practical principal	Material	Formal
Type of imperative	Hypothetical	Categorical

The attempt so far has been to show that what we are concerned with when we are concerned with *morality* is everything on the column on the right-hand side of the table. By showing us these links Kant can transfer to a further distinction. A hypothetical imperative is one that identifies a course of action as an adequate means to an end – it says that we ought to do some course of action in order to achieve some end. The 'goodness' of the course of action in such imperatives is only relative to the goodness of the end. If an agent does not desire the end then the course of action will not be good for them. So there is nothing inherently good about the course of action in hypothetical imperatives.

Kant wants to suggest that with categorical imperatives of morality, on the other hand, we understand that since the end is objective it is something that it is just good to do for its own sake. Any course of action essentially attached to the achievement of that end will be good then he thinks, not only as a means to an end but also for its own sake. Pursuing that categorical imperative is good, Kant thinks, not for what the desired end might achieve, but because it is an *end in itself* (4: 428).

Kant now makes a crucial move. If there is such a thing as morality at all, he claims, there must be something which can serve the role of an end in itself. The appropriate candidate for this thing which could be the source of why we must obey the necessary laws of morality is, he argues, the *human being*:

> But suppose there were something *the existence of which in itself* has an absolute worth, that, as *an end in itself*, could be a ground of determinate laws, then the ground of a possible categorical imperative, i.e. of a practical law, would lie in it, and only in it alone.
>
> Now I say: a human being and generally every rational being *exists* as an end in itself, *not merely as a means* for the discretionary use of this or that will, but must in all its actions, whether directed towards itself or to other rational beings, always be considered *at the same time as an end*. (4: 428)

Arguably, it is this simple thought – that human beings should be valued as ends in themselves and not used merely as means to an end – that has proven to be one of Kant's most influential and widely accepted claims. There is a clarity to the thought that if we use a person just in order to achieve some goal or end of our own, we are in that case in some sense not really treating them as a person at all. The value of that person for us in such a case is only insofar as they can be used to reach our desired goals. But in that case the value of the person is comparable to anything that would help us achieve those goals. In so doing, I reduce the value of the other person to the status of a mechanism or an instrument.

Imagine that someone wishes to open a locked door to which they lack the key. They have before them a crowbar and also a friend they know to be easily manipulated. Imagine they lie and tell the person that someone they love is behind the door and in need of their help, so they must break down the door. In such a case the person would have regarded their friend no differently than they regarded the crowbar, that is, as something that could be used to help them open the locked door. In treating one's friend in this way, one does not even engage in consideration about whether it is *right* to tell a person a lie in order to achieve a desired end – one is instead just considering the instrumental value of that person.

When Kant says that a human being is an end in themselves, he means that the value of a self-conscious and free agent is independent of whatever instrumental value they might have for the achievement of some desire. Kant argues that if this were not the case, then the only value human beings have to each other would be conditional on whether they could serve well as instruments or tools for the realisation of another's desires. However, it is a contingent matter what desires human beings have, in which case it would be a contingent matter whether a human being has any value at all – if the person could not be used as a tool for the satisfaction of any subjective end, then that person would have no value as a person.

Kant thinks that this is clearly not the case. We recognise that a person's value is absolute – it is not conditional on what effective use that person can realise. Furthermore, what we recognise when we recognise the absolute value of human beings as ends in themselves is their ability to engage *freely* and rationally in courses of action that they determine for themselves. When someone uses someone else as a means to an end, they do not respect that person's ability to determine for themselves what they *ought* to do, but rather they ignore that aspect of his nature and set him to work in an instrumental fashion.

Kant thinks that what is of absolute value in the human being as an end in itself is the human being's *rational nature*. It is this rational nature that we are referring to when we are referring to a human beings' intrinsic and non-instrumental value. Kant phrases the so-called *Humanity Formulation* (**FH**) of the Categorical Imperative as follows:

So act that you use humanity, in your own person as well as in the person of any other, always at the same time as an end, never merely as a means. (4: 429)

It is important to note exactly what Kant is claiming here. It is obvious that in most of our personal interactions we do in fact treat persons as a means to an end. When I ask someone I encounter on the street for directions, I have used that person as the means to my end of getting directions. There is of course nothing wrong with this. What would be wrong, Kant claims, is if the use of a person as a means to an end were incompatible with treating them as an end in themselves. He says that we must not 'merely' treat a person as a means to an end but be capable of 'at the same time' treating them as an end in themselves. To put it in the context of the claim about rational nature, I must not treat someone as a means to an end if by doing so I do not respect their ability to choose freely and deliberately or to determine their own actions. Thus, were I to grab a person and threaten them into giving me directions, I would have used them as a means to the same end as I would had I merely asked them for directions, but in this case I have not respected their right to rationally decide their own course of action in responding to me. By merely asking the person for directions I afford them the right to decline to give them to me, and though it would be strange and rude of them (and so perhaps a breach of etiquette), it would not be immoral of them to do so.

Imagine also a scenario where for some reason there was a moral dimension to the situation (say that I explain the life or death situation upon which getting directions depends). Were I to threaten the directions out of the person in this case, I would not give them the opportunity to either agree or refuse to give me the directions. In such a case, I have taken the issue of that person's moral agency off the table, since by forcing them to give me directions I have not even given them the *opportunity* to succeed – or perhaps fail – to do the right thing.

Secondly, one should note that Kant claims that one can treat one's *own self* as a mere means to an end and thereby fail to respect one's own rational nature. How this is so becomes clear as Kant returns to the previous four examples. Since the Humanity Formulation is supposed to be just an equivalent expression of the Universal Law Formulation, it must be the case that it can provide the same answer to each of the cases that we saw before. With regard to the perfect duty to oneself, i.e. the duty to preserve one's own life, Kant claims that the suicidal person's maxim of 'self-love' in effect amounts to them using their own living body as a tool to achieve a certain sub-jective end, namely that of ending their life. In so doing one would deprive one's future self of the capacity for self-determination but also use one's own self as a means to realising a contingently-held desired end. The human being though, Kant claims, 'is not a thing, hence not something that can be used *merely* as a means' (4: 429).

We can get a sense of how the Humanity Formulation provides similar results for each of the further examples. With regard to the false promise case, one is clearly using the person to whom one is promising falsely merely as means to the end of getting what one wants. In so doing, one deliberately neglects the other person's ability to determine for themselves what they ought to do (i.e. by granting *them* the choice to act on the basis of the knowledge that you might not consider your promise to be binding). Kant is similarly brief with regard to the imperfect duties to oneself and to others. With regard to the duty to cultivate one's talents, he claims that in not doing so, one fails to respect one's own rational capacity to enable the '*advance-ment*' of one's own humanity. With regard to the duty of benevolence to others, Kant claims again that although it is not contradictory to respecting humanity as an end in itself that I do not help others where necessary, it is not compatible with that demand insofar as I am com-mitted to positively and actively allowing for the full flourishing of humanity as an end in itself.

The next move that Kant makes in his analysis is to claim that insofar as a practical principle expresses a genuine categorical imper-ative at all (and remember that he has still not claimed to have proven yet that there really *are* such imperatives), it must be thought of as a moral law that the subject has somehow brought into being herself. This is a new connotation of Kant's moral philosophy, and frequently referred to in terms of the *autonomy of morality*. 'Autonomy' has many connotations, but here it means something like 'that which one makes binding upon oneself'. This contrasts with *heteronomy*, which we can understand as meaning 'those rules that are made binding upon oneself by something other than oneself'.

What does it mean to claim the morality must be autonomous? One might start by considering the common phrase 'he is a law unto himself'. When we say something like this we mean to say that the person is unpredictable and cannot be relied upon to follow the normal expected rules of behaviour. We might mean that for any given circumstance, that person will primarily decide for themselves what they want to do in that scenario, and only secondarily (if at all) consider what some set of rules or norms that others set down dictate that he should do. A second phrase we might consider – and one I mentioned before – is the notion of 'being true to oneself'. The context in which a phrase like this can make sense is when we are considering cases of struggles of conscience. A person might say 'the situation called for me to perform a certain action, but my conscience wouldn't allow it – I couldn't remain true to myself had I performed that act'. Here we have an intuitive understanding of what is being claimed here – while the standards set from others were relevant as guidelines for what the person should do, the primary authority was what that person deemed *for themselves* to be the correct course of behaviour.

Note also the previously mentioned phenomenon of the rational *authority* brought about by one's conscience. Once one has recognised what is the right thing to do according to one's conscience, only one's own conscience can change that opinion. If one thinks that *x* is not the right thing to do, nothing – no force whatsoever – can convince one otherwise. In these matters, one's own rational conscience has a kind of decisive trumping power over all other forces, including physical ones. Of course one can be threatened or cajoled into *performing x*, since we are all fallible creatures who frequently fail to do what we think is the right thing, but none of these can *change our mind* about what is just the right thing to do, even if we fail to do it. Recognition of a moral truth is like the recognition of a mathematical truth: once you understand that two plus three equals five, someone may subsequently put a gun to your head and demand that you deny it – and it might be reasonable do so, in the interest of self-preservation – but no threat in the world can make you believe that two plus three do not equal five or that infanticide is morally acceptable.

When Kant talks of the autonomy of morality, he means to capture some of these features. The domain of conscience has a kind of dignity and authority of its own, in that it has the power to be resistant to even the most powerful of the forces belonging to the physical domain – the rational domain is *autonomous* from the physical domain. One can, for example, sacrifice one's livelihood and even one's life on the grounds of conscience. When we engage in the CI-test, and recognise that a maxim is (say) demanded in accordance with the moral law, we view that result as binding upon us just because we view it as something that our own rational capacities have recognised as true. The result has this authority just because *we ourselves have given it* that authority, and once we have given it that authority, no 'external' power is capable of overthrowing it.

There is here a clear connection with Kant's methodology in his theoretical philosophy. In the *Critique of Pure Reason* Kant had advocated what is called his 'Copernican Turn', whereby he claimed that – although it initially sounds counterintuitive – the correct methodology for figuring out fundamental questions about the nature of the world must be pursued first by examining the basic contributions that the subject's own cognitive capacities make to the task of understanding that world. Thus, in order to understand how objective knowledge of the world is possible, we must first investigate the nature of the subject. Here too in the *Groundwork* we can see a similar strategy. Kant is what we might call an *objectivist* about morality: he thinks that there are such things as objective moral truths. However, he rejects what he would call *Transcendental Realism*: he would reject the claim that in order to access those objective truths we have to look to some external mind-independent domain (whether it be a theological domain, or a biological one, or whatever). Rather, we can – in fact we must – look only to the outputs of our own rational capacities in order to access those truths. Only then, Kant thinks, can we access a genuinely autonomous morality – looking to external domains as the source of moral truths will only ever produce a heteronomous morality.

We do not take the authority of categorical imperatives maxim to follow from any source other than what our own rational capacities demand of us to recognise as true. Note that were we to do so, the imperatives that result would not have the categorical quality that Kant has shown is the mark of the moral. If I performed an act because it was demanded by some external basis, such as the state's laws, or society's conventions, or the pushes of biological or psychological impulses, etc., I would express the demands that arose as follows: 'I must do x because it is demanded by y'. But if this were the case then the imperative produced would be merely hypothetical. As Kant puts it, 'the imperative always had to be conditional, and could not be fit to be a moral command at all' (4: 433). I would only *have* to perform x *if* I recognised the authority of y. Yet any of these candidates for the source of rational authority are dispensable – I can rationally determine that according to my own best judgement of what the right thing to do is, the demands of society or the state or even the behaviour that has naturally evolved in the development of mankind do not have any moral authority over my actions.

Were we to accept any of these demands we would be engaged in an attempt to justify a heteronomous morality, one where the authority of morality is explained from a source other than one's own rational will. Kant's claim ultimately is that the very idea of a heteronomous morality is a contradiction in terms. What it is to be engaged in moral thinking at all is to recognise the source of the right thing to do, and that source, Kant claims, must be an autonomous one. Kant expresses this claim by saying that only the rational will of the human being (with the capacity to respect the lawlikeness of demands of morality and considered as an end in herself) can provide this source of autonomy. It does so insofar as the human rational capacities do not merely recognise but in some sense set up or 'legislate' the moral law. It is, as Kant puts it, the 'idea of the will of every rational being, as a *universally legislating will*' (4: 431).

This leads Kant to outline a thought that can look paradoxical. On the one hand, morality's dictates are dictates that we view ourselves to be *bound* by – they tell us what we must do, and when we recognise them, we recognise that we have no option but to live by them if we are to act as genuine rational agents. On the other hand, if we want to view those dictates as genuinely moral dictates, it turns out that we must view them as laws that we ourselves have deemed to be binding. How can this be? When we say that someone is a 'law unto himself' we generally take it to mean that they tend to do whatever they want because they set the rules of behaviour for themselves. Here though it seems that Kant is claiming something similar – that agents set the rules of behaviour for themselves – yet the result is supposed to be the opposite. In the Kantian case we are supposed to see that *because* we set the rules for ourselves, we see that we are *not* able to do whatever we want.

Returning to the comparison with the recognition of mathematical truths, we can imagine that someone could choose to live their life by constantly denying the simple truths of arithmetic, however unwise that would be. But what he could not do is choose *to think* that those simple rules of arithmetic are false, no matter how much he wanted it to be the case. If he understands what the concepts in the judgement 'two plus three equal five' *mean*, then he must recognise the truth of the judgement irrespective of whatever course of behaviour he subsequently adopts with regard to them. The reason why he must recognise their truth is because his own rationality demands it of him. He cannot coherently deny to himself that two plus three equal five without denying that rationality has any hold on him at all.

With regard to the dictates of morality therefore, Kant is pointing to the phenomenon that the ultimate arbiter or judge of the correctness of a maxim is our own rational authority. We are bound by the nature of our own rationality to recognise the things that it says are the right thing to do as actually being the right thing to do. There is a sense then in which we are bound *by ourselves* to recognise what is right and similarly we bind ourselves to reject the things that are recognised as wrong, no matter how much we might like it to be otherwise. This, Kant thinks, points to another formulation of the Categorical Imperative, known as the *Autonomy Formulation* (**FA**). As Kant puts it:

According to this principle, all maxims are rejected that are not consistent with the will's own universal legislation. Thus the will is not just subject to the law, but subject in such a way that it must also be viewed as *self-legislating*, and just on account of this as subject to the law (of which it can consider itself author) in the first place. (4: 431)

The analogy drawn by Kant himself is with the political notion of self-legislation, of the setting up of laws for oneself. What does this mean though? We can imagine that when a state comes into being, it might declare its independence and bring itself into existence through the act of setting up a constitution. The constitution will define what the nature of the state is, who its citizens are, and so forth. In declaring their independence from other states, they will deem that the citizens of this state are subject *only* to the laws of that state and to no other external authority. The only legal authority they recognise is their own. Yet it is also the case that they will create for themselves their own governments, legislation, court systems, etc. Therefore, in setting up a constitution they declare that the citizens of the state will be subject to no laws *except* the laws that they themselves legislate. Therefore while they are in one sense 'a law unto themselves', in another sense they are also completely bound by those laws.

In fact, it is *just because* they themselves brought the laws in question into existence that they are in any way subject to those laws. Moreover, the citizens may cite the capacity for self-legislation as part of just what it is to be true to themselves, since it is this autonomy of self-legislation that defines what it is for them to be citizens of that state – it is part of what constitutes their political identity. Thus we can see that the concept of autonomous self-legislating agents is required by Kant to capture many of the features that he has already picked out as marks of what it is to be moral agent (i.e. the notion of the authority of rationality and conscience and the categorical bindingness of moral commands). As we shall see, however, autonomy has a further dimension, one concerning the notion of autonomous agents as *free* agents, which Kant will return to and which is crucial for the final stages of his inquiry in the *Groundwork*.

Finally, Kant turns to what is known as the *Kingdom of Ends Formulation* (**FKE**) of the Categorical Imperative. There is a sense in which this formulation must be presented by Kant last of all, since it can be understood as arising from a combination of the Autonomy Formulation and the Humanity Formulation. Each human being is an individual legislator of the universal law, and each human being is also an end in themselves. How then are we to think of a moral *society* of such beings? Kant thinks that the proper concept is that of a *kingdom*, by which he means 'a systematic union of several rational beings through common laws' (4: 433).

The vision Kant is asking us to imagine is one whereby each of our individual acts of legislation is performed in such a way that the rules produced are compatible with the rules produced by every other rational agent. Furthermore, the rules produced by any rational agent are such that they allow for every other agent to be treated always as ends in themselves and never as means to an end. A possible way of understanding the idea of a kingdom of ends is that of a kind of rational ideal of a perfect and harmonious system, where all the wrinkles that might stem from a person's individual circumstances have been ironed out, and where everyone's moral principles mesh seamlessly. The claim is that we cannot understand ourselves as moral agents in the way Kant has already described, i.e. as giving universal laws and as showing respect for persons as ends in themselves, without also committing to this ideal target of a complete system of harmonious rules.

Returning to the apparent paradox regarding self-legislation, we can see how Kant holds that in such a kingdom, any given agent would be properly described in two different ways:

A rational being, however, belongs to the kingdom of ends as a *member* if it is universally legislating in it, but also itself subject to these laws. It belongs to it *as its head* if as legislating it is not subject to the will of another. (4: 433)

Since one views oneself as bound by the moral laws one has self-legislated, then in the kingdom of ends, one would view oneself as just another member of the kingdom, whose will would have to accord with the will of every other member. On the other hand, if it is really a genuine kingdom of ends, then one's own rights as an end in itself would never be violated there, and it is then as if one would be the leader or ruler of that domain, since all the laws that hold there are the laws that one has inaugurated oneself. The vision of a kingdom of ends is one whereby every agent is a subject of the realm but also the ruler of the realm, since there is no law there stemming from some source other than one's own rational capacities, and thus no external authority that any agent must recognise.

Kant explicates the notion of a kingdom of ends by appeal to the distinction between something having a *price* and something having a *dignity*. Kant understands the former by saying that what 'has a price can be replaced with something else as its *equivalent*' (4: 434). It is not hard to see examples of what it would be to think of human beings in this way. If one thought that the value of a human being could be translated into something else and given a measurement, then one would have afforded humanity a mere price. This is of course literally so with the case of slavery and human trafficking. In viewing human beings as capable of being enslaved, we are in fact saying that their value as human beings can be adequately given in terms of (for instance) a cash value. In less literal cases though, we can see that when one treats a person as a means to an end in any situation, one is in effect affording them a price, albeit not a monetary one. If I use a person merely to achieve some further end, then I am giving a particular value to that person – their value in that case is translated into terms of their effectiveness as an instrument for the achievement of my ends.

When we afford something a dignity on the other hand, Kant claims that we are in fact denying that any such translation of its value into something else is possible. When something has a dignity it cannot be understood as valuable in any terms other than what it is. Kant says that something with a dignity is valuable in itself and as such incomparable with other valued things – it 'is elevated above any price and hence allows of no equivalent' (4: 434). We can see here the close connection Kant draws between the Humanity Formulation and the Kingdom of Ends Formulation, since what it is to treat someone as having an inner dignity is really just what it is to value someone as an end in themselves. Imagine the case of someone refusing to sell a family member. The potential buyer responds by offering more money. The person responds by saying that the family member is not for sale. The buyer then asks whether the family member might be for sale at a later date. The person at this point has to explain to the potential buyer that the reason why the offer of more money was refused is the same reason why the family member will *never* be for sale at any later date. The family member is a human being and has a value in itself, and that value cannot be compared to any amount of money whatsoever. The potential buyer has mistakenly taken human beings, beings that have an inner dignity, for things that have a mere price.

Of course there are many aspects of human beings that *do* have a price. As Kant acknowledges, any human being can have certain skills or abilities that he can trade in exchange for some recompense – we can and do treat people as a means to an end and allow ourselves to be treated as a means to others people's ends. We can do so in a professional capacity, of course, but we can also understand this in more simple ways. A particular person might be good company, and someone might value that person for their entertaining conversation. In such a case, one person values the other, but does not value the inner worth of that person – they do not thereby value that person in themselves. Why not? In this case one has valued the other *only* for something the person has that another person might provide as its equivalent – I might get good conversation elsewhere from another person. If *all* I valued the friend for was the enjoyment I got from their conversation, then the source of my valuing is really just the instrumental value there is for me in treating that person as a means to that end.

When one recognises another's fundamental dignity, it is because one recognises a quality in them that cannot be replaced by any other. This quality is simply that of their being a particular human being with their own rational will. Their own particular rational and free will is something that they themselves have alone, and it cannot be replaced by the rational and free will of any other. In the kingdom of ends therefore, every human being would afford each other a dignity based on a recognition of and respect for each other's inner worth as rational agents.

As was mentioned, Kant himself seems to recognise only three distinct versions of the supreme principle of morality – the Universal Law formulation, the Humanity formulation, and the Kingdom of

Ends formulation. When explaining the ultimate value of the dignity of a good will, he claims:

> It is nothing less than the *share* it obtains for a rational being *in universal legislation*, by which it makes it fit to be a member of a possible kingdom of ends, which it was already destined to be by its own nature, as an end in itself and precisely in virtue of this as legislating in the kingdom of ends . . . (4: 435)

Following this, Kant claims that the 'above three ways of representing the principle of morality are fundamentally only so many formulae of the selfsame law, one of which itself unites the other two within it' (4: 436). Why exactly the Autonomy Formulation is excluded from this list and why it is supposed to be that one formulation is supposed to unite the other two within it are somewhat unclear.

Kant returns to the topics of autonomy and heteronomy that he introduced earlier towards the end of the second section. Here he says again that autonomy is that feature of the will that makes it 'a law to itself' (4: 440). Another expression of the Autonomy Formulation is offered here:

> The principle of autonomy is thus: not to choose in any other way than that the maxims of one's choice are also comprised as universal law in the same willing. (4: 440)

As we have seen, it is only if the will gives itself its own laws that we can achieve autonomy of the will, and with it an autonomous ethics. If we take the moral law from anywhere else, Kant says, we will inevitably conclude with a heteronomy of the will, and a moral system of merely hypothetical imperatives. Kant puts the problem with a system of hypothetical imperatives quite forcefully – with such imperatives it is always the case that one expresses oneself as follows: 'I ought to do something because *I want something else*' (4: 441).

As Kant has repeatedly pointed out though, this is not how we think of moral commands – they present themselves as things worth doing not because they might afford one something else that one might want but just as worth doing for their own sake. If I understand that I ought not to torture because torture is morally wrong, then I cannot capture this thought in the form of a hypothetical imperative. I might say 'I ought not to torture because I will not to be punished by the law' or 'I ought not to torture because I will not to incur the disapproval of others', etc. But in expressing in this way I am not even *attempting* to express what I think is the *moral* status of torture. Here I am merely recommending a course of action one might take if one wills *other* things, such as avoiding disapproval or punishment. To see this, we can imagine someone who – for some bizarre reason – wanted to incur punishment from the law. In this scenario, the person might take the above hypothetical imperative as expressing the claim that torture is something that he ought to do, since it recommends that one should avoid it only because one wants to avoid legal punishment. Thus whether the hypothetical imperative is one one will follow depends entirely on whether the agent in question wills the relevant end.

This is plainly not how we think of morality. The 'oughts' in hypothetical imperatives just do not seem to be the same kind of moral 'oughts' that we are interested in when we are asking whether or not something is the right thing to do. Imagine a conversation where one person is asking another whether or not they should withhold some important information. Person A asks '*should* I withhold the information?' and person B responds with: 'well, if you want *x* to happen, then you ought to withhold the information; if you want *y* to happen then you ought not to withhold the information'. In such a case we can imagine our initial questioner complaining as follows: 'you're telling me what I ought to do relative to what I desire with regard to this or that outcome. But I'm not asking for that kind of pragmatic advice – I'm simply asking whether or not I *should* do it.' The miscommunication here concerns the respondent thinking that the questioner had asked for a piece of practical advice on what the consequences of their action might be, when what the questioner was interested in was whether or not the action was morally demanded. That the respondent missed that the question concerned the *moral* status of the act is seen by his expressing his response in terms of hypothetical imperatives. Had the questioner accepted the advice given she would have failed to consider the matter's moral status, and would be merely forming her intentions to act in accordance with whatever further ends she desired. In Kant's terms, she would be acting in accordance with a heteronomy of the will.

One achieves autonomy of the will when one forms one's intentions towards an action without any regard to whatever further ends might be achieved by that action, but instead considers only whether some end in itself might be achieved just by the very performance of that action. If I ask myself 'ought I to torture' and I respond that I ought not to torture because torture is morally wrong, then I have not referred to any advantage or disadvantage that may be accrued by performing the act – I have instead just considered the question of whether the type of action is in itself the kind of thing that is morally permissible.

As Kant comes to the end of the second section he examines some examples of heteronomous ethics, by dividing them into the class of ethics that have their values determined by empirical means and those that have them dictated by rational means. One might have thought that moral values that are determined by rational means are what Kant himself has been offering throughout the section; however, as we shall see, there are significantly different ways in which one can use reason in order to determine one's moral values.

Within the camp of empirical heteronomous ethics, Kant claims – unsurprisingly – that they cannot possibly serve as the basis for morality. It is important to see that Kant considers within this group so-called 'moral sense' philosophers (such as Hutcheson, for example). Very roughly, a moral sense philosopher might hold that one's morally correct behaviour can be determined by appeal to an innate sense that points one in the right direction without appeal to rationalisation or any particular calculation. In short they might claim that the capacity to sense the morally right thing to do is no more mysterious a capacity than any of the other capacities for sensation or judgement.

Kant acknowledges that such a sense would capture one of the intuitive aspects of moral judgement, namely its *immediate* character. Unlike a consequentialist, a moral sense theorist would have it that the correct apprehension of the moral state of affairs can just strike one as immediately as do the objects of vision. We might see in the visual sense that someone is attacking another person and also 'see' – in the moral sense – just as immediately that the act being performed is morally wrong. This feature – the immediacy of our moral judgement – is something that Kant thinks he has accommodated for with his characterisation of respect, which though immediate, is a kind of immediate *rational* recognition that something is the case, rather than a moral *sensation* of some mysterious kind.

He objects to moral sense theory, however, on the grounds of its failure to capture other different essential aspects of moral judgement, namely its objectivity and normativity. If we were to model our moral reactions on sensory feelings, they would have the character, Kant thinks, of only allowing for us to report as to how *we feel* with regard to a scenario. Grasping that something is morally wrong might be as immediate a phenomenon as, say, feeling that we are tired, but in other respects it is obviously different. When I immediately grasp that something is morally wrong I take myself as entitled to tell you that you too *should* appreciate the moral wrongness of the situation. I take my grasp of the scenario to be a grasping of an objective fact about morality with which I can make a normative demand of you – i.e. demand that you *ought* to act in accordance with a recognition of that objective fact. Plainly, though, I do not take this to be the case on any normal understanding of 'feeling'. I do not take it that I have grasped a normative truth about the world if I feel tired, for example. Similarly it would be very odd if someone were to say to another person that there is a normative demand that they ought to feel cold just because I do so. Yet these are reactions that we *do* take ourselves to be able to make off the back of our moral reactions.

Furthermore, even with more difficult cases, such as the feeling of disgust, which we do sometimes raise in regard to cases to which we have a moral response, we still take there to be an intuitive difference between reporting that feeling and reporting our moral response to the same situation. For example, one might think that it would make sense to us were someone to say of some state of affairs: 'I find it disgusting, and what's more, morally wrong.' Here we immediately understand that in saying that a state of affairs is disgusting we can be merely reporting the reaction of our feelings to the subject matter, and that more needs to be said with regard to the question of the moral status of that subject matter. More obviously perhaps, we can imagine someone saying: 'Personally, I find it disgusting, but morally permissible' – again, the status of our disgust reaction is frequently understood as irrelevant to the question of the moral status of the matter in question.

With regard to rational heteronomous ethics, Kant considers the notion of a system of moral values that hinges on a particular rational concept, that of *perfection*. Such a system might claim that we ought to behave in accordance with the characteristics of a perfectly virtuous agent. He mentions two criticisms of such rational heteronomous ethics. On the one hand, the system fails for the same reason that a system based on achieving happiness would that we saw earlier – the concept is just too vague or indeterminate to offer us any particular guidelines on just how to behave in order to achieve perfection. Secondly, Kant claims that if someone tried to thicken up the concept of perfection so that it might offer some specific guidelines, they would only do so by smuggling in some already accepted moral notions. For example, one might claim that in becoming perfect one must become perfectly virtuous, but again this is only a suggestion one might accept so long as one already had a concept of virtue and already thought that becoming virtuous was something worthwhile. In such a case therefore, we would *already* know what morality is – i.e. becoming virtuous – and thus the concept of perfection would be doing no extra work in our understanding of morality.

Kant rejects another version of rational heteronomous ethics, namely that of theological ethics. One might base a system of moral values based upon whatever is the output of God's will. Kant provides a dilemma for such a conception. On the one hand, we might judge that we ought to do God's will because God's will is good. In this case we would be in the same situation as before, in that we would already require a notion of the morally good to apply to God's will in the first place. But if we already know what is good from other means then we do not require the idea of its being endorsed by God in order to recognise it as such. On the other hand, if we do not assume that God's will is good, then we would be advocating that one should follow God's will just because it is God's will and that one ought not disobey God. But, as Kant points out, this gets our moral motivation all wrong: we would in that case be performing an act not because it is morally good but because it is the kind of thing that God approves of, and that might benefit us with his good favour in an afterlife;

similarly, we might refrain from performing an action not because it is wrong but because it is the kind of thing God disapproves of, and might punish us for doing. This kind of reasoning, i.e. prudential reasoning, is precisely what we *do not* do when we reason morally. We recognise things as right or wrong independently of what we think anyone – even God – might judge about them. To base our moral system on divine approval would, Kant thinks, 'be directly opposed to morality' (4: 443). (We must remember here though that Kant himself was a man of deep personal religious conviction and his views on the relation between morality, faith and happiness are in fact more complicated than those that are just indicated in the critique of theological ethics in the *Groundwork*).

In all of these cases Kant holds that the resulting heteronomy can be explained by the fact that the human will has allowed itself to be determined by some 'object' or target – whether it be happiness, perfection, God's will, society's conventions, etc. As he points out though, if we attempt to reason to moral values in this way, then the universal status of our conclusions will always be conditional on whether or not the 'objects' we have in mind are the universal targets of human beings and specific enough to offer guidance. But in each of these cases then we would need more rules telling us why everyone ought to have just *these* targets as the correct objects of the will. Someone might ask 'should everyone do *x*?' and a reply might come 'well, it's God's will/society's convention/etc.', but all this does is say that *if* everyone wills to respect God's will or society's conventions, *then* everyone should do *x*. As such, the commands of morality would be reduced to mere hypothetical imperatives, and if they are to be raised to a higher status then we will need a new story about why everyone must respect God's will or society's conventions, etc.

Kant thinks that what we are really looking for when we ask 'should *everyone* do *x*?' is the mark of the moral as the universal and necessary law, i.e. as categorical. It is this abstract feature that is the only valid thing we have to go on when trying to determine what is the right thing to do, and cannot be achieved by the identification of any hopeful moral 'objects'. Kant returns to the form/matter distinction in explaining this notion. When trying to determine the morally correct thing to do, we must ignore the 'matter' of our maxims – that is, the particular 'objects' that our maxims might be concerned with – and instead focus exclusively on their categorical *form*. Is my maxim the kind of thing that I can coherently demand that every free and rational agent ought to do? Does my maxim have the *form* of the moral law? This, it turns out, is what Kant thinks we are really asking ourselves when we ask ourselves what we ought to do.

Third Section – *Transition from the metaphysics of morals to the critique of pure practical reason*

As Kant has repeatedly stated, everything that has come so far in the *Groundwork* has been directed at answering the question of the definition of morality: of unpacking or revealing what the very idea of morality involves. As such, he has so far only been committed to establishing the conditional claim: *if* there is such a thing as morality, *then* it must be a system of categorical imperatives. What he says he has not even attempted to do yet is to show that there even *could be* such a thing as morality – to show that morality is in fact possible. (I have suggested earlier that Kant sometimes talks as if there is no question as to whether or not morality exists, since 'common moral judging' in fact reliably shows it to be the case – this may be Kant's own personal belief, but he certainly does not think that he has established or proven this to be the case.) In the third section of the *Groundwork*, Kant finally turns to this question. We saw at the end of the second section that the notion of an agent having an autonomous will is supposed to be bound up with the possibility for that agent to act morally. Kant begins the third section with a sub-section entitled 'The concept of freedom is the key to the explanation of the autonomy of the will' and this states exactly the essential part of his strategy for showing that morality is genuinely possible.

As we have seen, Kant has contrasted two domains of explanation, the rational and the natural or physical. While all physical beings must obey the laws that govern the domain of natural explanation, some of these beings must also obey different laws, ones that govern the domain of rational explanation. We can imagine a creature lacking the capacity for explicit self-consciousness (such as a fish, for example) engaging in all sorts of actions, but when we characterise those actions we characterise them exclusively as actions that come about just by virtue of their being different kinds of physical responses to causal stimuli. The fish does not deliberate as to what it *ought* to do, but rather merely reacts to the sensations that are stimulated in it by its environment. As such, the fish is an agent that acts by virtue of 'alien causes *determining* it' (4: 446). By 'alien causes' Kant means that the actions that are brought about by causes outside of the fish's own will (if the fish has a 'will' at all).

We have also seen that if there is such a thing as morality, it must involve autonomy of the will, where that is understood as involving the possibility of actions that are brought about not by the pushes and pulls of desire or inclination for some external 'object', but rather because there is some standard that we may set for ourselves and that can serve as the basis for a different kind of action. At the beginning of the third section, Kant defines what it is for an agent to have a free will in terms of these two domains of explanation and the different kinds of *causality* that belong to each. When I act unfreely, it is because I act on account of the forces of 'alien causes' determined by nature; when I act freely, it is because my actions are brought about independently of any influences of the laws of nature.

As he admits, this definition is negative: it says that I act freely when I bring about results without any outside physical influences. Nevertheless, Kant has already noted some crucial points, not least of which is that he holds that our free will is to be characterised as a kind of *causality*. We intuitively think of the law of cause and effect as something that pertains exclusively to the physical domain. However, the concept of causality is in fact much broader, in that one can think that effects can be brought about without any special appeal to laws of nature. In a court of law, for instance, a judge may decide in favour of one of the applicants, and in so doing bring about a judgement. We would intuitively think that the cause of the judgement was the judge's simply deciding it so, without saying that there was an especially relevant law of nature in operation here. Similarly, as we saw, when one asks 'why did you do that?' we are not asking for the identification of the physical cause but rather what we are looking for involves an account of what *reason* brought that event about.

Although the power of free will is then for Kant a kind of non-natural causality, this does not mean that it is merely another way of describing things that happen. For Kant, the causality of the will is a power human beings have literally to bring about events without there being any law of nature that determined that it must happen or must not happen. Moreover, Kant thinks that any kind of causality, if it is to be a genuine kind of causality at all, must be one that acts in accordance with necessary laws. Therefore, while natural causality operates in accordance with the laws of nature, since free will is itself a form of causality, it too must act in accordance with necessary laws.

This is at first a quite counterintuitive notion of freedom. We often think of freedom negatively, as the capacity to perform actions without the presence of any constraints. If asked what it means to be free, many of us would describe it as a capacity to act without being held back by this or that force. Kant is clear that this is not the notion of freedom that he is arguing for. Freedom is not the ability to be completely unconstrained by any rules whatsoever – it is not to be 'lawless' altogether, but rather it is only the state of being unconstrained by *alien* laws, that is, from laws from outside the will itself. Since the will is a kind of causality, and all causality involves necessary laws, it must be that to have a free will is to act in accordance with the necessary laws that a will sets for itself. (In a sense it is only now that one can appreciate Kant's initial characterisation of ethics as the 'science of the laws of freedom' with which he began the *Groundwork*.)

Thus Kant has identified the capacity of a will to be autonomous – that is, to be capable of acting as a 'law unto itself' with the very capacity of free will. The capacity to exercise our free will therefore is realised when we act autonomously, and we act autonomously only when we act in accordance with the moral law:

Thus if freedom of the will is presupposed, morality along with its principle follows from it, by mere analysis of its concept. (4: 447)

In the second section Kant argued that the concept of morality could be examined to show that the concept of a good will involved the notion of a will whose maxims could be willed as universal laws. This involved showing that these two notions – that of a good will on the one hand, and that of universalised maxims on the other – were connected together. However, the manner in which those notions are connected was not through a strict procedure of logical deduction. Kant does not think that we can start with a premise about the definitions of the concept of a good will and, through a series of simple deductive steps, show that this notion entails the notion of morality as a system of categorical imperatives.

Had he done so, he would have been able to establish the moral law *analytically*, in that he would have followed the methodology of a traditional rationalist, who simply tries to unpack or analyse what is logically entailed within the definition of a given concept. While Kant has been engaged in an examination of the concept of morality, and while he has appealed essentially to reason as the means of performing this examination, his method has been different from traditional rationalism in important respects. Kant holds that although there are genuine connections between concepts (for example between the concepts *morality* and *freedom*), he does not think that these connections can be discovered just through the process of analysing the definitions of either of these concepts into their constituent parts.

Instead, Kant is engaged in what I have called procedural rationalism. The idea regarding procedural rationalism is that there are essential features of concepts that can be discovered by reason only through an examination of how those concepts are *used* in procedures of reasoning, and not through a mere analysis of their definitions. Therefore Kant has tried to show connections between the common notion of morality, and the idea of the form of a law, of a person as an end in itself, of the idea of autonomy, etc., by examining the ways in which we use or operate with the concept of morality. The CI-test is a procedure for uncovering properties of a maxim that are not evident to reason at first glance, but are only revealed when we put them through that test.

For this reason Kant claims that the connection that he has established between the concepts of a good will and the concept of a universal maxim is not analytic but a *synthetic* one. For Kant, a synthetic connection is one that is made when we see that two concepts are properly joined together in virtue of some further explanation of that connection. In effect then, for all genuine synthetic connections, we require *three* elements, and in the case of the concepts of a good will and the supreme principle of morality, Kant has already indicated what that third element must be:

Such synthetic propositions are possible only by this, that both cognitions are bound together by their connection with a third thing in which they are both to be found. The *positive* concept of freedom provides this third thing . . . (4: 447)

As Kant goes on to explain, if freedom in this positive sense (i.e. as a type of causal power to bring about actions) is the essential connecting thing for these concepts, then it must be the case that we can attribute this conception of freedom to all possible rational agents, since morality is supposed to hold for all possible rational agents. As he puts it, freedom 'must prove it as belonging to the activity of rational beings endowed with a will as such' (4: 448).

Kant's analysis has brought him to a crucial point. He has attempted to show that the concept of morality is in fact essentially connected with the concept of freedom in this positive sense. What this means is that if one wishes to show that morality is in fact possible, one must address the metaphysical question of whether or not human beings are genuinely free. The question of the relationship between freedom and morality has a long history in philosophy, but here Kant brings that relationship to the fore. Nowadays the philosophical problem is a familiar one, and we can express it in Kant's terms: if we are creatures whose actions are always determined exclusively by the physical laws of nature, such that no free self-conscious deliberation is ever the primary cause of our actions, then how can we ever be genuinely morally responsible for those actions? By characterising our practical reasoning as a mere response to physical stimuli, we threaten to render our moral values as entirely heteronomous, as merely automatic mechanical responses to some external 'object'. As such, if we lack genuine freedom of the will, it seems that the reasoning produced by our will always shall always take the form of hypothetical imperatives, which fail to characterise the essential features of morality entirely.

We would expect at this point in the *Groundwork* a shift from moral philosophy to metaphysics, since Kant has seem to argue that what is required to ground a system of categorical imperatives is a metaphysics of freedom. However, that is precisely what we do not get. In fact, at this crucial point of the *Groundwork*, Kant expresses his commitment to the idea that proving a metaphysics of freedom is not in fact possible. So far, very little of what Kant has been arguing has relied upon any of the claims regarding Transcendental Idealism made previously in the *Critique of Pure Reason*, but now it is important to return to those claims. Recall that Kant had argued there that while we can know necessary truths about the world of appearances, there is a further domain of explanation, that of things in themselves, about which we cannot know anything at all. Secondly, Kant argued in the *Critique* that while every human person has an empirical self that is perfectly knowable, each person is also a thing in itself that is entirely unknowable. Thirdly, Kant argued that the power of freedom is a power that ultimately is a feature of the person as a thing in itself. Kant is therefore already committed to the claim that the capacity of human beings to bring about actions through a causal power of freedom is not something that we can ever know or prove to be the case. He does say, however, that we can at least *think* that freedom is possible. Freedom, if it is possible, must be entirely special, since on this model it is a power whose causes originate in one domain – the unknowable domain of things in themselves – while its effects, i.e. actions themselves, are manifested in the physical domain of appearances. As such, the idea of a transcendental power of freedom is one that crosses over between two otherwise entirely distinct and separate domains or worlds.

It might seem that the *Groundwork* has argued itself to a disappointing anti-climax, since the book has moved towards showing that for the possibility of morality to be established, the causal power of freedom *must* be established, only to conclude that this conception of freedom *cannot* in fact be established. The worry might be that the *Groundwork*'s aim of establishing morality is destined to fail on its own terms. At this point though, Kant makes a vital (and controversial) move that he claims avoids this consequence. He claims that, although we cannot prove that we are in fact free in this positive sense, it is still the case that we must act *as if* we are free in this positive sense, and that this necessity of acting as if we are free in this positive sense is in fact sufficient to establish morality:

Now I say: every being that cannot act otherwise than *under the idea of freedom* is actually free, in a practical respect, precisely because of that; i.e. all laws that are inseparably bound up with freedom hold for it just as if its will had also been declared free in itself, and in a way that is valid in theoretical philosophy. (4: 448)

What is it to act 'under the idea of freedom'? We can get some grip on this notion by thinking of just the common practice of describing the psychology of our actions. Could it be the case that we can coherently ascribe a moral action to ourselves as chosen by our will and yet at the same time *deny* that we are free? Could I really say for instance: 'I choose to help others when they are in need (but my choice is not one I freely undertake)'? What would I mean when I say 'I choose to help others' if I in fact think that I am not free in this positive sense to do so? Of course, someone might have a gun to my head, or I may have a compulsive disorder that forces me to perform such actions, and I might for some reason say 'I choose to help others', etc., but in such scenarios it would surely be the case that I understand that what I am doing here is in an important respect *not* a real choice for me.

Kant's claim is that it is a matter of a kind of practical necessity that in order to understand our actions as genuine actions at all, we must characterise them as actions resulting from *genuine* acts of choice, and to understand the latter, we must understand them as the results of a free will. This, of course, is not a proof that we *are* free wills – if sound, it only secures a weaker conclusion to the effect that we must *think* of ourselves as free if we are to think of ourselves as agents. Kant's next step is to claim that for the purposes of the possibility of moral behaviour there is no difference between the claim that we *know* that we are genuinely free and the claim that we must *think* of ourselves as genuinely free. Both, Kant claims, are equally sufficient to establish morality, and as such the fact that we lack a proof that we are genuinely free does not undermine the project of the *Groundwork*:

I follow this route – of assuming freedom only, sufficient for our purpose, as made the foundation by human beings in their actions merely *in the idea* – so that I may not incur the obligation of proving freedom in its theoretical respect as well. For even if this latter point is left unsettled, the same laws that would bind a being that was actually free yet hold for a being that cannot act otherwise than under the idea of its own freedom. Here we can thus liberate ourselves from the burden that weighs upon theory. (4: 448, note)

Kant acknowledges the limitation of this conclusion. He had promised that in the third section he would 'corroborate' the supreme principle of morality, having only examined the concept in the preceding sections. Yet here it can look like he has to admit that he cannot in fact corroborate the moral law, if that were to mean what we intuitively think it means, i.e. to prove it to be true. Instead, all Kant has shown is that the concept of morality is inextricably linked with the concept of freedom, or, as he puts it, that they are 'reciprocal concepts' (4: 450). As such they stand or fall together: if the concept of morality is a genuine one (by which I mean if it is possible that there is actually something to which the concept refers) then it must be the case because the concept of freedom is a genuine one. We must at least assume that the concept of freedom refers to something possible, and so we must at least assume that the concept of morality refers to something possible.

In a sense then, Kant's conclusion can seem like a merely conditional one, in that it is only if we are committed to the genuineness of one concept that we can defend the genuineness of the other. Kant describes the situation as being committed to an argumentative circle:

There appears at this point, one must freely admit, a kind of circle from which, as it seems, there is no escape. We take ourselves to be free in the order of efficient causes so as to think ourselves under moral laws in the order of ends, and we afterwards think ourselves as subject to these laws because we have ascribed to ourselves freedom of will; for freedom and the will's own legislation are both autonomy, and hence reciprocal concepts; but precisely because of this one of them cannot be used to explicate the other or to state its ground, but at most only to reduce to a single concept, for logical purposes, representations of just the same object that appear dissimilar . . . (4: 450)

Again, one might be concerned that at this crucial final stage of the inquiry, the claim is being made that not only can we not establish that we are free, but that we do not need to do so.

Kant's reasoning is somewhat obscure again here, but it is at least clear that he thinks that the fact that the proper explanation of morality requires something like Transcendental Idealism, with its distinction between appearances and things in themselves, and the claim that we can only know the former, to be an actual *advantage* of the analysis that he has given of the relationship between freedom and morality. Kant goes on to elucidate the distinction between the domain of appearances and the domain of things in themselves. He claims that the distinction is an intuitive one, since it means just the distinction between how things appear to us and how they are 'behind' those appearances (Kant is not here offering an argument for Transcendental Idealism, but rather just making an appeal to the intuitiveness of some of the basic notions behind the theory).

One way of thinking of the distinction is that appearances relate to how our cognitive capacities are affected, and things in themselves are the ultimate explanatory ground that bring it about that we are affected in the ways that we are. When we think of the distinction in this way, Kant claims, we already have a sense as to how and why the human person might also be both an appearance and a thing in itself, since the human person has the capacity not just to be affected but also to bring about certain things. The human agent has the causal capacity (or at least the agent must think of herself as having this capacity) to bring about actions beyond the influence of the effects of external physical causes. If we think of 'appearances' as corresponding to 'that which is affected' and 'thing in itself' as 'that which brings about effects' then we can see that the notion of the self as a thing in itself provides a plausible model for the source of the capacity for the autonomy of the will.

All we can know about the self is the empirical self, the self that is affected, has sensations, etc. In this way the self belongs to what Kant calls '*the world of sense*', i.e. the domain of appearances. However, we can also experience the power that the self has to bring about actions through its own causal capacity of freedom, and there must be, he claims, some aspect of the self corresponding to the source of this power. That aspect of the self must exist in the domain of things in themselves, or as Kant puts it, the '*world of understanding*' (4: 451). Since the domain of things in themselves is unknowable according to Transcendental Idealism, and since there is an aspect of every free self that is a thing in itself, it must be the case that there is an aspect of the self that is unknowable.

Kant thinks that this Transcendental Idealist picture in fact suits our ordinary picture of the spontaneity of our free wills in action. When we decide to pursue a course of action freely, we are not, it seems, in any conscious contact with the source of our metaphysical freedom. Rather, we become aware of our freedom only through the outputs or results of our exercising that power in producing actions. Thus I am aware of my freedom only through my awareness of my free actions, e.g. I freely choose to raise my hand, and I am aware of my exercise of my freedom through my sensory awareness of how my body is affected by my power of freedom. This is just an awareness of the effects of that causal power, however – what I never have any direct awareness of is the causal power of freedom itself.

The claim then is that a philosophical system whereby the power of freedom originates in the domain of things in themselves, but whose outputs or effects are realised in the domain of appearances, is just what is required in order to explain the ordinary phenomenon of free action. This is the kind of system that Transcendental Idealism in fact offers. Given that we are never directly aware of the origin of our free will, we might conclude one of two things. On the one hand, we might conclude that we have no awareness of our actual causal power of free will because there is no actual causal power of our free will, and that the notion that we choose freely is in fact an illusion. If this is the case, and if Kant's analysis of the reciprocal nature of the concepts of freedom and morality is correct, then it follows that the concept of morality is an illusion also.

On the other hand, we might conclude that the reason why we have no knowledge or even awareness of the causal power of our freedom is not because there is no such thing, but rather because there *is* such a thing, only that it is the kind of thing that lies in a domain beyond the human capacity for knowledge. Kant's system of Transcendental Idealism shows how it is possible that, *despite* our lack of awareness of the causal power of freedom, this does not entail that it is a mere fiction, since it can be that our free will is in fact an actual but unknowable thing in itself. As such, we do not have to infer from the unknowability of freedom to the fictional nature of morality.

In Kant's view, only Transcendental Idealism can still explain how morality is still possible. It does this by offering the human being two different perspectives or 'standpoints' from which he can understand the nature of his actions:

On account of this a rational being must view itself *as an intelligence* . . . as belonging not to the world of sense, but to that of understanding; and hence it has two standpoints from which it can consider itself, and recognise laws for the use of its powers, and consequently for all its actions; *first*, in so far as it belongs to the world of sense, under laws of nature (heteronomy); *secondly*, as belonging to the intelligible world, under laws that, independent of nature, are not empirical, but have their foundation merely in reason. (4: 452)

Kant concludes that this Transcendental Idealist picture of the self removes the worry he himself raised earlier regarding the possible circular reasoning. He does not assume the idea of freedom just so that we may suppose the idea of morality; instead, he claims that we must think of ourselves as creatures belonging to a completely different domain than the empirical world of sense if we are to think of ourselves as rational agents with a will at all; it then follows, he claims, that if we think of ourselves as creatures of that domain of the understanding we must think of ourselves as autonomous and hence moral agents.

Kant offers what he calls a 'deduction' (4: 454) of the moral law. In the *Critique of Pure Reason*, Kant offered a 'Transcendental Deduction' of the concepts of the understanding (such as substance and causation), called the Categories, and he claims here that the deduction of the moral law is in some ways analogous to that argument. The Transcendental Deduction is itself a notoriously difficult and obscure argument, making it difficult to determine what exactly the analogy that Kant is drawing here is. A very rough description of the Transcendental Deduction is that it attempts to show that the concepts of the understanding, i.e., the Categories, are valid by showing that they are necessary conditions of the possibility of experience. The argument claims that if the Categories did not apply, then experience as we know it would not be possible. So for Kant we can start with a very simple observation – for instance, that experience of a world of apparent objects in time is possible (something that even a sceptic would accept) – and show that in order for *this* to be possible, it must also be the case that certain concepts, such as those of substance and causation, etc. must already be presupposed as applying validly. Thus the sceptic is committed to the validity of these concepts if she is to accept the coherence of ordinary experience, since the former is a necessary condition of the possibility of the latter.

Considering the analogy in this way suggests one possible way of reconstructing Kant's argument here (once again, there are many competing interpretations with regard to this part of the *Groundwork*). Here he seems to be arguing firstly that there is an ordinary type of experience that everyone – even a sceptic – must accept; secondly, he is arguing that in order for that ordinary type of experience to be possible, we must assume that we are free agents capable of acting in accordance with laws of morality. Kant claims that the ordinary type of experience that anyone must accept is the capacity to express to oneself that something *ought* to be the case. What is it to think that something ought to be the case? What are the necessary conditions of this kind of thought making sense?

In answering this, Kant asks us to think of two possible situations. In the first case, we imagine that we are purely rational agents, beings who *only* existed in the world of understanding, without any aspect of our existence belonging to the world of sense. What would it be *like* to be such a being? We would have no desires or inclinations that would threaten to disrupt what the laws of freedom determine for us to do. In such a case we would not be capable of ever *failing* to do the right thing, since it is only the interruption of desires and inclinations that lead us astray from the laws of reason in the first place. But it is clear that we *are* beings who are capable of failing to do the right thing – we think that when we express a moral 'ought' we are describing something that should happen, but not that it is something that necessarily *will* happen. If we were only beings belonging to the world of understanding then laws of freedom would rule completely and would determine everything that will happen (4: 454). Human beings are physically embodied, finite and fallible moral agents and as such clearly are not agents who belong completely to the world of understanding, just by virtue of the fact that the possibility of moral failure is a real possibility for us.

On the other hand, we might imagine what it would be like if we were beings who existed *only* in the world of sense. What would *this* existence be like? We can see that the situation would in fact be quite similar to the one that arises if we were beings who existed only in the world of understanding. Since the world of sense is determined *completely* by the physical laws of nature, if we were creatures who existed only in this domain, we would then be creatures whose actions were entirely determined by those physical laws. If we were to think of ourselves only as beings in such a world, we would think that everything that we do is determined only in accordance with the laws of nature. But in this imagined scenario, we would always obey the laws of nature and again would not even have *the very idea* of there being any laws that we might on occasion *fail* to obey.

When we say to ourselves that something ought to happen – for example, when I say that I ought always to tell the truth – I am describing myself as a being whose actions are not completely determined by laws of nature, for in that case I would think of all my actions as simply happening necessarily in accordance with laws of nature. Neither, however, am I describing myself as a being whose actions are completely determined by laws of the understanding, because in that case all my actions would happen necessarily in accordance with laws of freedom. Rather, when I say that I *ought* to do something, I take it that in accordance with one set of laws – the laws of morality – that thing *must* happen, but in accordance with another set of rules – the laws of nature – it might *not* in fact happen. This is exactly how Kant described the difference between natural and moral philosophy back in the Preface:

> [Natural philosophy describes] laws according to which everything happens, [moral philosophy describes laws] according to which everything ought to happen, while still taking into consideration the conditions under which quite often it does not happen. (4: 388)

Kant's claim is that the very meaning of the moral 'ought' depends on a very specific necessary condition, namely that we must take ourselves to be beings that exist *both* in the world of sense and the world of understanding. If the meaning of the 'ought' is that something in one sense must happen but in another sense need not happen, then we require, Kant thinks, a distinction between two different domains to explain how the 'ought' gets this specific meaning.

Kant's 'deduction' of the principle of morality might then be reconstructed as follows. Even the sceptic must at least acknowledge the initial coherence and distinctness of our ordinary idea of the moral 'ought'. This 'ought' has two distinctively normative features. The first of these is what we might call its *necessitation condition* – it makes some kind of demand upon us and in so doing tells us that something *must* occur. The second is that it allows what we might call a *failure condition* – I ought to do *x* in this moral sense only if it is possible that I might actually fail to do *x*. Kant's claims is that in order to explain *both* these normative features we have to presuppose that the agent belongs to two different domains at the same time: the existence of the self as a rational thing in itself in the world of the understanding is necessary to explain how we are affected by the demand of the moral ought; the existence of the self as a physical being in the world of sense is necessary to explain how there is sometimes failure to meet those demands (i.e. when the demands of freedom's laws are interrupted by the sway of desires and inclinations). Therefore, the moral 'ought', and with it the categorical imperative, is possible only if we are agents both of the world of sense and of the world of understanding.

Kant thinks – controversially perhaps – that we cannot deny to ourselves the appeal of being a good person or recognition of the possibility of moral self-improvement. Even 'the most hardened scoundrel' (4: 454), he claims, can recognise the appeal of moral goodness, despite their ingrained resistance to pursuing it. The only way to understand this recognition, Kant claims, is to imagine the behaviour that we would engage in if we were purely rational beings existing in the world of understanding. Of course, as we have seen above, this is not something that is in fact possible for us if the moral 'ought' is to make sense, but it is, Kant claims, what we think of when we think of becoming a morally better person. When we ask ourselves – of course from the perspective of beings who in reality exist at least partially in the world of sense – what it would be for us to do what we ought to do, we are in one sense trying to imagine what we would do if we were beings only inhabiting the world of the understanding:

The moral ought is thus one's own necessary willing as a member of an intelligible world, and he thinks of it as an ought only in so far as he considers himself at the same time as a member of the world of sense. (4: 455)

Kant's claim here is the same as in the deduction described above: the moral ought gains its meaning only under the condition that we think of ourselves as being members of two domains or worlds at the same time. The Transcendental Idealist picture of the human being, as existing both as appearance and as thing in itself, offers a metaphysical account that satisfies this demand.

Kant also uses this claim to resolve what he takes to be an apparent contradiction. This contradiction lies in the fact that it is our single capacity of human reason that pushes us to think of pictures of our existence that are in straightforward tension with each other. Reason can be used for what Kant calls '*speculative purposes*' (by which he means for the purposes of our various inquiries into the structure of nature) but also for '*practical purposes*' (by which he means for the purposes of our moral inquiries). It is the same single capacity of human reason that tells us that as human beings our actions are entirely determined by the physical laws of nature *and* at the same time that as human beings our actions are independent of the determination of the physical laws of nature. This tension Kant calls the risk of a 'dialectic of reason' (4: 455). How is it possible that reason's compelling us to both these contradictory claims can be acceptable? Kant says that one's philosophy must offer a means of resolving or defusing this tension:

It must therefore presuppose: that no true contradiction can be found between freedom and natural necessity of just the same human actions, for it cannot give up the concept of nature, any more than that of freedom. (4: 456)

The situation is a difficult one, since Kant must claim (a) that the possibility of freedom is required for the possibility of morality, (b) that the possibility of freedom cannot be comprehended and (c) that the concept of freedom is in straightforward tension with the concept of natural necessity. As he acknowledges, the risk is that one would simply abandon the very idea of freedom, and with it the substantial kind of morality attached to it. Kant takes himself thus far to have resolved the tension by showing that we can avoid a contradiction between the possibility of freedom and the possibility of natural necessity if they are thought of as concepts properly referring to two different domains or worlds. The contradiction arises only if we are to think of them as referring to a single world.

Yet the absence of a contradiction is not a positive reason to accept it (4: 456). The task of resolving this apparent contradiction is not a task of moral or practical philosophy, Kant claims, but instead one of theoretical or speculative philosophy, and to make room, so to speak, for the possibility of moral philosophy. The resolution of the tension is based on elements Kant has already presented and relates to the claim about the necessity of acting under the idea of freedom. It is a universal and necessary feature of a human agent – that is, an agent capable of conscious deliberation on her ability to act – that she must represent herself as an agent that can be moved by two different types of causes that correspond to two different aspects of her nature (that are nevertheless tied together in her being). In order to represent oneself self-consciously as an agent, therefore, one must represent oneself as an agent existing with a foot in each of two worlds:

A human being who considers himself in this way as an intelligence thereby puts himself in a different order of things and in a relation to determining grounds of an entirely different kind, when he thinks of himself as an intelligence endowed with a will, and consequently with causality, than when he perceives himself as a phenomenon in the world of sense (which he actually is as well) and subjects his causality, according to external determination, to laws of nature. (4: 457)

If we accept Kant's claim that what it is to be a being in the world of sense is to be merely a self as it appears, then we can understand his further claim that when the self is conscious of itself as 'an intelligence endowed with a will' then she is aware of herself as a possible thing in itself (even if this awareness does not constitute *knowledge* of oneself as a thing in itself). Thus Kant claims that a metaphysical division of the world into appearances and things in themselves is required if we are to make sense of the two aspects of our being – as physically determined *and* as rational and free – of which we are capable of being conscious.

In the *Critique of Pure Reason*, Kant had introduced a distinction that is crucial to the feasibility of his Transcendental Idealist project. Kant holds that all knowledge claims are made possible through the combination of both concepts – which are the basic elements of acts of thinking – and intuitions, by which he means particular representations of individual objects. Only if we have both in combination can we have knowledge. However, things in themselves are, according to Kant, things of which we can have no possible intuition, in which case it follows that we cannot make any knowledge claims about them. For Kant a knowledge claim is one that must target some *object*, and for an object to be latched on to by our minds, we require both concepts and intuitions. We are unable to have an intuition of any object as a thing in itself and so lack one of the vital components required for knowledge claims about them. Kant does hold though that we can nevertheless make many claims about things in themselves, which, although not meeting the standard of *knowledge*, can count as important and perhaps necessary judgements for us. Admittedly, it is a difficult question as to just what kind of status these claims are supposed to have, but Kant is clear that we are capable of *thinking* certain claims about things in themselves, i.e. just through our use of concepts alone, even if we are not capable of *knowing* those claims to be true.

We can see then that Kant's solution here turns on a knife-edge. It is part of his Critical Philosophy that we must assume that there is a world of things in themselves as well as a world of appearances; however, he also claims that the world of things in themselves is unknowable. It might appear here, though, that in claiming that awareness of our rationality and freedom makes available a sense of ourselves as things in themselves, he is thereby breaking his own rule regarding knowledge of things in themselves. However, Kant is clear that throughout this section he is not making any knowledge claims about things in themselves. He is arguing here that human beings must *represent* or *think* of themselves as things in themselves if they are to make sense of themselves as even rational agents at all. He thinks this is enough to respond to the sceptical character who might want to deny that we are in fact genuinely free. Kant's strategy is to claim that we can never know that we are in fact genuinely free but that even the sceptic – who surely thinks of herself as a rational agent – is at least committed to representing herself as genuinely free if she is thinking of herself as a rational agent at all. So while in one sense Kant is accepting a severe limitation to our knowledge, he thinks that not only are the ideas of a domain of freedom and a domain of natural necessity non-contradictory, but we are rationally committed to thinking of ourselves as having a foot in each domain. This, Kant concludes, is both the most and the least we should expect for the practice of moral philosophy.

At this point of the *Groundwork*, Kant appears to return to this important distinction between thinking of things in themselves and knowing them in order to explain what occurs when one considers one's own self as a thing in itself:

> By *thinking* itself into a world of understanding practical reason does not at all overstep its boundaries; but it would if it wanted to *look* or *sense* itself *into it*. (4: 458)

Kant returns to the themes of the *Critique* here, stating that practical reason would overstep its bounds if it attempted to target a particular '*object of the will*' from the domain of the understanding. As we have seen, Kant is clear that our practical reason does not attend to any particular 'matter' when considering moral action but rather can only consider the form of the moral law. This is not to say that there might not be an 'object' of the will – in the form of one of the laws of freedom that govern morality – merely that those laws, if real, must reside in a domain that is beyond the reach of our capacity for knowledge.

Kant then concludes that it is the proper understanding of both the nature of our practical reason and morality that on the one hand we must presuppose the concept of this different world, but that this presupposition is limited to being a necessary *thought* rather than a necessary knowledge claim. Thinking that we partially belong to a world of understanding is an unavoidable and indispensable thought, but it can only ever retain the epistemic status of a thought to which we are committed and as 'a *standpoint* that reason sees itself necessitated to take outside appearances, *in order to think of itself as practical*' (4: 458).

Since the possibility of the moral law has been identified with the possibility of freedom, it follows that the attempt to know about the fundamental basis of why and how the moral law is possible is identical with the attempt in metaphysics to establish why and how the power of free will is possible. In the *Critique of Pure Reason*, this had been one of the several metaphysical concepts that Kant claimed to have shown not to be impossible but merely unknowable. While we cannot *prove* that our metaphysical freedom is real, he thinks, it is also the case that for the same reasons we cannot *disprove* that our metaphysical freedom is real.

This conclusion alone might not hold much sway with the opponent Kant calls the *fatalist*, i.e. someone who holds that determinism is true and free will impossible, with the consequence that there is no genuine individual moral responsibility for their actions. However, we must recall that Kant holds that the idea of freedom is inescapable even for the fatalist. Thus Kant's position maintains that we cannot know that freedom is possible, but neither can we know it to be impossible, *and* we must in practice think as if it *is* possible. This combination of claims is enough, he thinks, to rebut the sceptic or fatalist, and proceeds without attempting to make knowledge claims about the domain of things in themselves.

Kant thinks that the only area where human beings *are* capable of providing any kind of explanation is the domain of appearance and with the laws of physical nature that govern it. Therefore we should not even *attempt* to explain something whose origin lies in the domain of things in themselves, since this is in effect an attempt to go beyond the proper domain of explanation itself. As a result, someone who wishes to defend Kant's moral theory is always in a position whereby they must argue their case not by providing a proof that explains how the moral law is actually objectively real, but instead has to act as a kind of border guard against those who try to claim that freedom is impossible or that the moral law is *not* objectively real:

But where determination by laws of nature ceases, there all *explanation* ceases as well, and nothing is left but *defense*, i.e. warding off the objections of those who pretend to have looked deeper into the essence of things, and therefore boldly declare freedom to be impossible. (4: 459)

This kind of position is arguably what makes Kant's practical philosophy 'Critical' – it is directed not just towards substantiating certain philosophical claims and refuting others but also in identifying what kinds of philosophical claim are capable of being substantiated or being refuted and which kinds of claim are beyond the realm of possible substantiation or refutation. The fundamental basis of the moral law – the explanation of how freedom itself is possible – is in Kant's view one of those philosophical claims that is beyond the realm of definitive substantiation or refutation.

Kant also feels the need to clarify the status of his original claims about the centrality of the feeling of respect for the moral law. Here he argues that the phenomenon of 'taking an interest' in the moral law is also itself impossible to explain. It will follow from the fact that the origin of the feeling of taking an interest in the moral law is related to the domain of things in themselves that it too cannot be explained. However, as with the moral law itself, the phenomenon of taking an interest in the moral law, i.e. being motivated to act in accordance with it, can be defended from those who would try to deny its reality or claim that its origin lies elsewhere than in the domain of things in themselves.

Kant provides this defence by characterising some of the features of rational understanding on the one hand and feeling on the other and pointing out that neither can alone suffice to characterise what it is like to take an interest in the moral law. On the one hand, it cannot be a matter of simply having reason recognise that something is the case, on the basis that it is just not within the capacity of our rational faculty to generate feelings as a source of motivation. The recognition of an 'ought', Kant thinks, is the recognition of a kind of causality upon ourselves such that we feel motivated to act just by virtue of that recognition. Kant has already argued in the first *Critique* though (and here he is in agreement with empiricists such as Hume) that causality is not something that can be explained by appeal to reason alone. Therefore, if the feeling of taking an interest is the experience of a kind of causality, it cannot be a causality that is accounted for solely by our reason.

On the other hand, neither can experience account for the characteristic features of interest in the moral law. Kant denies that our rational understanding can fully explain the phenomenon but there is an *aspect* of the phenomenon that is entirely rational, and that is (as we have already seen) the order of explanation or direction of fit between the recognition that the moral law is valid and its being a source of motivation for action. We could imagine that an empirically minded moral sense theorist might hold that we ought to act in accordance with whatever the output our feeling of moral sense indicates. This, according to Kant, gets things the wrong way around: when we act out of a sense of obligation, we do not think that something is made true by virtue of our having a sense of obligation about it, but rather that we have a sense of obligation generated by our rational recognition that something is true. This rational recognition must come from some *other* source than the reasonings of our self as appearance, however, since as we have seen above, that aspect of our reason is also incapable of explaining the interest that we take in morality:

Just this much is certain: it is not *because the law interests* us that it has validity for us ... but the law interests because it is valid for us as human beings, since it arose from our will as an intelligence, hence from our actual self; *but what belongs to mere appearance is necessarily subordinated by reason to the constitution of the thing in itself.* (4: 460–1)

By the concluding paragraphs of the *Groundwork*, Kant has brought us to what he calls 'the supreme boundary of all moral inquiry' (4: 462). He has attempted to show that, while we can determine what we ought to do in particular cases of moral unclarity by appealing to the CI-test, with regard to a more general question, namely 'how is morality itself even possible?', he has shown that its answer lies beyond the limits of human explanation. The questions 'how is morality possible?', 'how can pure reason be practical?' and 'how is free will possible?' are all shown to be in fact equivalent, and the impossibility of providing an answer to one entails the impossibility of providing an answer to the others.

This conclusion – of showing that a kind of answer to moral inquiry is impossible – should not be thought of as a negative result, Kant thinks. The real damage that human beings have done to each other throughout history has not infrequently been precipitated by an assumption that one or the other (or both of them) has gained genuine insight into the 'inner essence of things' and has thereby acquired a kind of moral authority for their actions. The appeals to purely empirical considerations or to some kind of supreme yet comprehensible rational authority are not only futile searches, but can often generate consequences that are, as he gently puts it, 'harmful to morals'. Kant's aims are always motivated by his awareness of human beings' capacity for cruelty and intolerance on the one hand, but on the other lies his optimism that their inherent rationality can provide a corrective power of benevolence and fairness in the face of that threat.

It is just as much the case though that although reliance upon our rational capacities is part of the solution in moral philosophy, the difficulty of achieving results has in the past stemmed from our over-confidence in our own intellectual capacities. It is a mistake to think a certain special type of inquirer might have privileged access to the fundamental and eternal truths of morality. Human beings are *all* finite and fallible creatures, and our method for determining how we ought to treat one another has to respect that fact. Kant's moral philosophy is ultimately directed towards the aspiration of goodness that human beings can show to one another while maintaining a sense of humility about our capacity to understand even our own nature. He claims that he has shown that we cannot comprehend the origin of the moral law, but he has shown *why* this is the case – he has shown that we can 'comprehend its *incomprehensibility*, and this is all that can reasonably be required of a philosophy that in its principles strives up to the boundary of human reason' (4: 463).

A moral philosophy that claims to reveal insights about the very nature of things in themselves is perhaps not the kind of moral philosophy we ought to be endorsing. Were we to claim such insights we perhaps would not be living in a world where it is even possible that we could ever fail to do the right thing; but the value that the moral 'ought' has for us is that it designates something that we think should happen but that is capable of not happening. The importance of moral action for us, and the reason why we value those who manage against the odds to live a morally good life, both stem from the constant threat that we might fail to live up to our own moral standards. In a world where we had infallible access to all the moral *answers*, the risk of failure would disappear and with it that special dignity we put upon the task of living one's life with sensitivity to the *questions* of morality.

Kant has attempted to do what he thinks is the most that any moral philosophy can, which is to show what it is that we are in fact valuing when we recognise someone's actions as morally worthy. What we are in fact valuing is their acting out of a sense of duty and obligation towards what their own rational consciousness demands of them. Similarly, what we are recognising is someone's refusal to treat another merely as a means to some end; we are recognising instead their insistence on respecting that other person as an end in himself or herself. We are recognising persons as having a dignity in their own right, simply by virtue of their existence as human beings. We are recognising that what a person is holding to be the right thing to do is simply a result of what their own rational conscience demands of them, and as refusing to allow that understanding to be bullied by any other external standard. Ultimately we are recognising the hopeful possibility that a person's moral actions might be of a kind that can be incorporated into a world where every human being can coexist with every other in accordance with shared standards of decency and respect.

3. Study Aids

Glossary

Analysis
: The method whereby concepts are investigated through decomposition into their constituent parts.

Analytic
: A judgement is analytic if the subject concept already contains the concept in the predicate position as part of its definition.

A posteriori
: A representation is a posteriori when it is acquired or justified exclusively by appeal to the evidence of experience. For Kant, a posteriori representations only ever offer the basis for knowledge of contingent truths.

Appearance
: That which concerns the representations of the subject. Kant defines empirical reality relative to appearances, and so 'appearance' does not have the connotation of indicating something false (e.g. as when one says 'it merely appears that way').

A priori
: A representation is a priori when it can be justified or known independently of experience. A priori claims always involve claims to necessary truths and are those that are known with certainty.

Autonomy
: The capacity of a will to determine itself independently of external influences. An agent acts autonomously when she acts in

	accordance only with the rules that she has freely set for herself as morally demanded.
Categorical	That which is concerned with absolute or unconditional necessity.
Category	A type of concept whose function it is to make experience possible. In Kant's theoretical philosophy, substance and causation are two fundamental Categories.
Cognition [*Erkenntnis*]	Cognition is the knowledge human beings can have of the world by virtue of their ability to combine both concepts and intuitions in judgement.
Critical	That which concerns the possibility of knowledge through an examination of the powers and limitations of the subject's own cognitive capacities.
Deduction	A justification of a concept through the demonstration of its role as a necessary condition of the possibility of some form of experience.
Duty	The obligation to perform or not perform a task on the basis of one's recognition of principle alone.
Form	The element within our maxims that concerns its potential to be formulated in a lawlike way.
Freedom	The causal power of the will to determine its own actions for itself autonomously.
Heteronomy	The feature of a demand that is set by standards or sources of authority other than an agent's own rational capacities.
Hypothetical	The form of reasoning that characterises a rational means to achieve a particular desired end.
Humanity	The feature of individuals that characterises their absolute value and worth independently of any instrumental value they may have.

Imperative	A rule that expresses a necessary course of action.
Inclination	Motivations afforded by appeal to the needs generated by our desires.
Intuition	An immediate representation of a single individual object.
Kingdom of Ends	A formulation of the Categorical Imperative that envisions a community of agents co-existing harmoniously, with the characteristic of each member of the community having also the status of the sovereign of that community.
Law	A rule that holds necessarily and universally (i.e. without exception) for an entire domain.
Matter	The particular content of a maxim as it relates to some particular circumstances or conditions.
Maxim	A subjective rule or plan adopted for a course of action.
Practical	That which relates to the ethical or political. In general, Kant's practical writings concern different ways in which human beings' free nature is managed.
Respect [*Achtung*]	A recognition of the truth of the moral law combined with the motivation to act in accordance with it.
Self-legislation	The act of setting a rule, standard or law as binding upon oneself by virtue of the fact that it has originated only from oneself and not from any external source of authority.
Synthesis	The act of combining two representations through the identification of some third common element that can be seen to connect the two.
Synthetic	A judgement that concerns the connection of two concepts where their connection is

understood as being based on some other ground than mere definition.

Theoretical	That which concerns the possibility of knowledge of the world.
Thing in itself	The source or explanation of things in the world insofar as that explanation lies beyond the capacity for human cognition.
Will	The practical reasoning capacity of the agent and her ability to form intentions to act.

Types of Question You will Encounter

1. Exposition

Interpreting Kant's position can be a challenge in itself, and frequently students will be asked simply to make clear some central notion within his thought. In so doing, one should be able to consider a range of contexts in Kant's primary texts where that notion is to be found, and to offer an analysis of those references. An ability to consider the relationship between Kant's understanding of that notion and the way it is understood by other philosophers (e.g. Descartes, Hume, etc.) will often be required.

2. Issues in Kant Interpretation

As we have seen, many of Kant's notions are difficult to interpret, and frequently complicated disputes arise. An essay may concern the question of how to adjudicate such disputes (e.g. 'How ought we to interpret Kant's notion of self-legislation?').

3. Modern Philosophy Problems

As with nearly all great works within the history of philosophy, Kant's are written in the context of – and sometimes in direct response to – the works of other great philosophers. Students may be asked to situate Kant's thought with regard to that of philosophers such as Hobbes, Hume, Hutcheson, Rousseau, Shaftesbury and others.

4. Philosophical Problems

The *Groundwork* addresses many contemporary philosophical issues in both ethics and metaethics. Students may be asked to abstract from the specific context of the *Groundwork* and to examine questions from a 'Kantian' perspective (even if not exactly from Kant's own perspective).

Common Assessment Criteria

The quality of your essay will be judged according to criteria that may include some of the following:

1. The clarity of the writing. Pay special attention to the construction of a clear structure for the essay. Most importantly perhaps, indicate at the beginning of the essay exactly what the thesis (the claim you will be arguing for) is and how you will proceed to argue for that thesis.
2. Demonstration of the student's broader understanding of the issues, and manifestation of a grasp of the connections between Kant's views and those of other philosophers, both historical and contemporary.
3. Evidence of engagement with the primary material. The *Groundwork* is a classic in the history of philosophy, and the essay must show evidence of the student's familiarity with the text itself.
4. Ability to use secondary sources. The challenge for one's use of secondary sources is to use them in a judicious way. This means identifying the central points made by those sources and reporting their views clearly and concisely. The stronger essays will be those where the student shows both understanding and independence of thought with regard to that secondary material.

Tips for Writing about Kant

1. References to the *Groundwork* frequently take the form that have been used in this book, with the *Akademie* reference system – e.g. 4: 406 – being given after quotes or references. References to the *Critique of Pure Reason* are usually made with the 'A/B' references

– e.g. A248/B304 ('A' refers to the first edition of the *Critique*, and 'B' refers to the second edition. All good translations of the First *Critique* will use this system). Most of Kant's other works are usually referenced with the standard *Akademie* reference.

2. Pay close attention to the nature of the essay question asked. Frequently questions will be phrased in such a way as to require both an exposition of a particular aspect of Kant's thinking and a critical portion, where you will be invited to offer an evaluation of that topic and to offer reasons in favour of your view. Be careful to structure your essay to allow sufficient space for both tasks.

3. Take care when deploying Kant's terminology. 'Idea', 'concept', 'motive', 'incentive' etc. all have technical meanings. Try to avoid using these words in their ordinary meaning so as to avoid confusion for the reader.

4. Try and approach Kant's writings charitably. Kant is a philosopher who frequently challenges the reader with the obscurity and demanding nature of his writing. His views can also appear counterintuitive on first encounter and thus invites disagreement. However, one of the reasons why Kant is one of the acknowledged great philosophers is because there is always potential to find some reasonable motivation for each claim that he makes – one should always approach the text with the ambition of discovering the most plausible reasons that Kant may have had for his views.

5. Having said that, it is important to always keep in mind where you might disagree with Kant's position. A good essay on Kant will always reflect a student's personal engagement with the material and a good way of doing this is attempting to clarify exactly one's own point of disagreement or departure from that material, even if it ultimately constitutes a relatively minor issue.

Bibliography

Works by Kant

Kant, I. (1996a), *Practical Philosophy*, trans. and ed. Mary Gregor, Cambridge: Cambridge University Press.

Kant, I. (1996b), *Religion and Rational Theology*, trans. George di Giovanni, ed. Allen W. Wood, Cambridge: Cambridge University Press.

Kant, I. (1997), *Lectures on Ethics*, trans. and ed. P. Heath and J. B. Schneewind, Cambridge: Cambridge University Press.

Kant, I. (1998), *Critique of Pure Reason*, trans. and ed. Paul Guyer and Allen W. Wood, Cambridge: Cambridge University Press.

Kant, I. (2012), *Groundwork of the Metaphysics of Morals*, intro. Christine Korsgaard, trans. Mary Gregor and Jens Timmermann, Cambridge: Cambridge University Press.

Other Sources

Allison, H. E. (1990), *Kant's Theory of Freedom*, Cambridge: Cambridge University Press.

Allison, H. E. (2011), *Kant's Groundwork for the Metaphysics of Morals: A Commentary*, Oxford: Oxford University Press.

Ameriks, K. (2000), *Kant and the Fate of Autonomy: Problems in the Appropriation of the Critical Philosophy*, Cambridge: Cambridge University Press.

Baron, M. W. (1995), *Kantian Ethics Almost without Apology*, Ithaca, NY: Cornell University Press.

Beck, L. W. (1960), *A Commentary on Kant's Critique of Practical Reason*, Chicago: University of Chicago Press.

Engstrom, S. (1992), 'The Concept of the Highest Good in Kant's

Moral Theory' *Philosophy and Phenomenological Research* 52: 747–80.

Guyer, P. (ed.) (1992), *The Cambridge Companion to Kant*, Cambridge: Cambridge University Press.

Guyer, P. (ed.) (1998), *Kant's Groundwork of the Metaphysics of Morals: Critical Essays*, Lanham, MD: Rowman and Littlefield.

Guyer, P. (2000), *Kant on Freedom, Law, and Happiness*, Cambridge: Cambridge University Press.

Herman, B. (1993), *The Practice of Moral Judgment*, Cambridge, MA: Harvard University Press.

Hill, T. E. Jr. (1991), *Autonomy and Self-Respect*, Cambridge: Cambridge University Press.

Horn, C. and D. Schönecker (eds) (2006), *Groundwork for the Metaphysics of Morals*, Berlin/New York: Verlag Walter de Gruyter.

Korsgaard, C. (1996), *Creating the Kingdom of Ends*, Cambridge: Cambridge University Press.

O'Neill, O. (1989), *Constructions of Reason: Explorations of Kant's Practical Philosophy*, Cambridge: Cambridge University Press.

Paton, H. J. (1971), *The Categorical Imperative: A Study in Kant's Moral Philosophy*, Philadelphia: University of Pennsylvania Press.

Reath, A. (2006), *Agency and Autonomy in Kant's Moral Philosophy*, Oxford: Clarendon Press.

Schneewind, J. B. (1998), *The Invention of Autonomy*, Cambridge: Cambridge University Press.

Sedgwick, S. (2008), *Kant's Groundwork of the Metaphysics of Morals: An Introduction*, Cambridge: Cambridge University Press.

Sullivan, R. (1994), *An Introduction to Kant's Ethics*, Cambridge, New York: Cambridge University Press.

Timmermann, J. (2007), *Kant's Groundwork of the Metaphysics of Morals: A Commentary*, Cambridge: Cambridge University Press.

Timmermann, J. (ed.) (2009), *Kant's Groundwork of the Metaphysics of Morals: A Critical Guide*, Cambridge: Cambridge University Press.

Timmons, M. (ed.) (2002), *Kant's Metaphysics of Morals: Interpretative Essays*, Oxford: Oxford University Press.

Wood, A. W. (1999), *Kant's Ethical Thought*, New York: Cambridge University Press.

Wood, A. W. (2008), *Kantian Ethics*, Cambridge: Cambridge University Press.

Index

Printed and bound by CPI Group (UK) Ltd, Croydon, CR0 4YY

21/01/2025

01823422-0002

.